AMERICA'S CASTLE

AMERICA'S CASTLE

*The Evolution of the Smithsonian Building
and Its Institution, 1840–1878*

KENNETH HAFERTEPE

SMITHSONIAN INSTITUTION PRESS

City of Washington, 1984

This book was edited by Ruth W. Spiegel
and designed by Alan Carter.

Library of Congress Cataloging-in-Publication Data

Hafertepe, Kenneth, 1955–
    America's Castle.

    Bibliography: p.
    Includes index.
    1. Smithsonian Institution Building (Washington, D.C.)
2. Smithsonian Institution—History. I. Smithsonian
Institution. II. Title.
Q11.S8H3 1984   507′.4′0153   83-600216
ISBN 0-87474-500-4

The paper in this book meets the guidelines
for permanence and durability of the
Committee on Production Guidelines for
Book Longevity of the Council on Library Resources.

TO CHARLES AND GLORIA HAFERTEPE

Contents

❈

Illustrations

Foreword

✣

THE death of the rather obscure English scientist James Smithson in Genoa, Italy, in 1829 and the resulting mysterious bequest of a half million dollars to the United States set in motion the long and arduous steps that eventually resulted in the chartering of the Smithsonian Institution by Congress in 1846. It was in that year that New York architect James Renwick, Jr., designed the Smithsonian Building, with its eight romantically soaring Norman towers, chapel, porte cochere, rose windows, and hand rusticated sandstone façades. Fondly known as "The Castle," this landmark stands today as a living symbol of the world's largest complex of museums as well as one of the most significant American centers for both cultural and scientific research. The story of how the Castle originated, the complicated process by which this enormous five-part-plan building was erected, and the political infighting involved with the building's early use sets the stage for understanding the history of the Smithsonian Institution.

The author, Kenneth Hafertepe, has produced an outstanding scholarly work through his careful survey of long-neglected letters, diaries, account books, and minutes of the Smithsonian's governing body, the Board of Regents. Few Gothic novels of the nineteenth century or even American soap operas of today could capture the intrigues, Machiavellian politics, and scandals relating to the first thirty years of the Castle's history. Mr. Hafertepe's vivid depiction of the power struggle between one of the original Smithsonian regents (and the author of the Smithsonian charter), Congressman Robert Dale Owen of Indiana, and the Smithsonian's first Secretary, Professor Joseph Henry, is only one of the colorful episodes unraveled here. Other highlights include the controversial architectural competition for the Castle, the battle by Charles Jewett to change the major thrust of the Smithsonian from the promotion of major scientific research into a national library, the disastrous fire of 1865, and Secretary Henry's ultimate success in solidifying his political and executive control of the fledgling institution. Secretary Henry's objections to James Renwick—as chronicled here by Mr. Hafertepe—may have been colored by the Secretary's dislike for the building: what Henry considered its impractical design and the extravagant and unnecessary cost. Perhaps Henry's criticism should have been directed toward Renwick's choice of contractors rather than the design of the Castle itself. Unfortunately, James Renwick's papers have not survived, so that certain questions are left unanswered.

Under the leadership of the Smithsonian's eighth secretary, S. Dillon Ripley, the Castle has undergone a major restoration since 1964. During the 1930s, 1940s, and even 1950s, the Castle slowly deteriorated. At that time, when Victorian architecture and decor were popularly considered in "poor taste," this landmark lost much of its historic character: most of the Castle's Victorian furniture and chandeliers were replaced with "improved" steel desks and fluorescent lights, the great oak doors with their massive Gothic iron-strap hinges gave way to aluminum and plate glass, and the hardwood floors were covered with linoleum. During the past two decades, however, restoration has proceeded full steam. Every year witnesses the replacement of long-altered windows, steps, doors, roofs, towers, and even hardware. Dozens of rooms have been furnished with American Victorian chairs, desks, tables, and other authentic furnishings from the period 1840–1880.

Not only has the Castle undergone a physical metamorphosis, but the many cultural and academic activities that were common to the building during Joseph Henry's stewardship have come home again. The project to locate and publish the Joseph Henry papers is constantly shedding new light on the nineteenth-century design and function of the Castle. The establishment of the Woodrow Wilson International Center for Scholars in the upper floors and turrets of the Castle in 1970 has lent to the building an academic character which has been missing during most of the twentieth century. The major project now underway to build two underground museums in the old south yard of the Castle will foster a new appreciation for the culture and art of both African and Near Eastern civilizations.

This new Quadrangle so aptly identifies with James Smithson's legacy "for the increase and diffusion of knowledge among men." The Castle has indeed come full cycle. *America's Castle* is a most important addition to our increased knowledge of architect James Renwick's creativity as well as to the overall unfolding Smithsonian saga.

JAMES M. GOODE
Keeper of the Smithsonian Building

Acknowledgments

M ANY are the names that helped to shape the Smithsonian Building. Some arts may be solitary, but not architecture. Nor, for that matter, is the writing of a book a solitary venture; my debts have multiplied at a rapid rate. This list will inevitably miss a few of the names that helped to shape this work, but my gratitude is none the less for it.

Although my interest in architectural history awakened during my senior year at Georgetown University, that interest had no academic outlet and no direction until I began work in American Civilization at the University of Texas at Austin under Dr. William H. Goetzmann. His encouragement and advice as the project grew from a seminar paper to a Master's Thesis and then far beyond have been of crucial importance. Dr. Jeffrey L. Meikle served as a reader of the thesis, and his comments on that and later versions of the manuscript have improved it immeasurably. Many long conversations with Professor Drury Blakeley Alexander of the School of Architecture of the University of Texas have greatly increased my knowledge of architectural history, and have been most pleasurable in the process. Seminars and conversations with Dr. Robert M. Crunden of the American Civilization Program and Dean Elspeth D. Rostow of the Lyndon B. Johnson School of Public Affairs have been most influential on my thinking. Dr. Crunden has generously added his comments to some parts of the manuscript.

The Joseph Henry Papers project at the Smithsonian Institution is, simply put, a researcher's paradise. Dr. Nathan Reingold and his staff were most generous in allowing me to roam through their impressive collection of Henry materials, and in providing their expert help whenever I needed it. I am therefore deeply indebted to Dr. Reingold and to Dr. Marc Rothenberg, Dr. Arthur Molella, Ms. Kathleen Waldenfels, Ms. Joan Steiner, and Ms. Beverly Jo Lepley.

Helpful criticism of the manuscript has come from several other quarters of the Smithsonian. Mr. James M. Goode, the Curator of the Smithsonian Building, has lent his vast expertise and was also of great assistance in procuring many of the illustrations for the volume. Dr. Wilcomb E. Washburn, Director of the Office of American Studies, gave a very careful reading of the manuscript and has improved it accordingly. Dr. Cynthia Field of the George Washington University has been most generous in sharing her time and her research on the Castle. I look forward to her own volume on this subject.

Thanks must also go to Dr. John Morrill Bryan of the University of South Carolina, who provided me with a Xerox of the letter from Robert Mills to Robert Dale Owen, which is in the South Carolina Historical Society; Dr. Bryan's biography of Robert Mills promises to be most fascinating. Conversations with Dr. Arthur Channing Downs, Jr., of Newtown Square, Pennsylvania, were most instructive, and I eagerly await his volume on A. J. Downing. Mrs. Selma Rattner, of New York, who is at work on a monograph on James Renwick, Jr., offered a number of criticisms, some of which I have accepted. For the many helpful suggestions by all my readers and by the Smithsonian Institution Press, I am grateful; of course, ultimate responsibility for my interpretation—and my missteps—remains solely with me.

The staff of several archival centers have contributed their expertise to my search for materials. I must name Mr. C. Fred W. Coker, the Head of the Reference and Reader Service Section of the Manuscript Division, the Library of Congress; Mr. George Perros and Mr. Ed Schame of the National Archives; Mr. Thomas Dunnings of the New-York Historical Society; and Mrs. Josephine M. Elliott and the staff of the Workingmen's Institute, New Harmony, Indiana.

Generous permission to quote from archival materials has been granted by Her Royal Highness Elizabeth II, queen of England, and by the following institutions here: the Academy of Natural Sciences, Philadelphia; the American Antiquarian Society, Worcester, Massachusetts; the American Philosophical Society, Philadelphia; the Boston Public Library; the Avery Architecture Library, Columbia University; the Gray Herbarium, Harvard University; the Houghton Library, Harvard University; the Huntington Library, San Marino, California; the Indiana Historical Society, Indianapolis; the New Hampshire Historical Society, Concord; the New York Botanical Garden Library; the New-York Historical Society; the Princeton University Library; the Rutgers University Library; the Bailey Library, the University of Vermont; the Sterling Memorial Library, Yale University; and above all, the Smithsonian Institution Archives.

Over the past three years the folks at the Smithsonian Institution Press and I have shown each other a great deal of patience; I'm still not sure who needed it more. At any rate I must single out for thanks the designer of this book, Alan Carter, and especially my editor, Ruth W. Spiegel, who wields *The Chicago Manual of Style* with dexterity and diplomacy.

Financial support for this project has come in the form of a Smithsonian Graduate Fellowship for the summer of 1979, a Robert Lee Blaffer Trust Fellowship for January 1982, and a blank check from my parents. Beyond the financial support which my parents, Charles and Gloria Hafertepe, have provided over the years, their love and encouragement have been inspiring. This book is really theirs.

Introduction

❧

U PON his return to Washington, D.C., in 1851 after an absence of some nine years, the sculptor Horatio Greenough spent an evening wandering along the banks of the Potomac. The United States Capitol stood to the east, illuminated by the moon which rose above the clouds. Greenough continued to stroll as the river curved to the southeast, when "suddenly, as I walked, the dark form of the Smithsonian palace rose between me and the white Capitol, and I stopped. Tower and battlement, and all that medieval confusion, stamped itself on the halls of Congress, as ink on paper! Dark on that whiteness—complication on that simplicity!" The building frightened him. He sensed "a certain mystery" about the towers and belfreys that made him uneasy. "This is a practical land. They must be here for something. Is no *coup d'état* lurking there? Can they be merely ornaments, like the tassels to a University cap?"[1]

The Smithsonian Castle, four years under construction and another four from completion, held no invading army that night. Eventually it would house a university professor and his family, and, from time to time, provide shelter for a small number of men making up the vanguard not of revolution but of scientific research. Yet even though no coup d'etat lurked beneath that sandstone exterior, the political process that resulted in the decision to build a castle had been a fierce struggle, with momentous consequences for the future of the Smithsonian Institution.

James Smithson had willed his small fortune to the United States for the founding at Washington of an institution to bear his name, and dedicated, somewhat ambiguously, to the "increase and diffusion of knowledge." Robert Dale Owen, a visionary congressman from New Harmony, Indiana, gave some definition to the phrase in his bill to create the Smithsonian Institution. He called for a library, a museum, an art gallery, lectures, and all the facilities necessary for

scientific research. Having guided the bill to passage, Owen natu-
rally was appointed to the Board of Regents of the Institution, and
quickly persuaded his colleagues to erect a building in the Romanesque, or as he preferred to call it, the Norman style. Owen had in
mind not only a Norman structure but also a preferred architect and
a particular plan even before the election of the chief executive officer of the Institution.

Joseph Henry, the professor of natural philosophy at Princeton,
was elected as the first Secretary of the Smithsonian three days after
a subcommittee chaired by Owen declared its preference for the
Norman design of James Renwick, Jr., of New York. Henry was
adamantly opposed to any expenditure that did not facilitate scientific research, and opposed in particular to a large building that
might become a library, an art gallery, or a museum. This put him
in immediate conflict with the plans of Robert Dale Owen. In the
midst of the week-long debate that had concluded with the adoption of Renwick's plans by the Board of Regents, Henry wrote to
his wife that "unfortunately Owen is struck with an architectural
mania, and were it not for this the [Regents favoring the building]
would be in the minority."[2] Mania or not, Owen was determined to
see the building go up.

The architect, James Renwick, Jr., and the other entrants in the
competition for the Smithsonian Building had been given an extremely detailed program, including floor plans and elevations drawn
by David Dale Owen, the brother of Robert Dale Owen. Renwick,
like the others, dutifully followed the wishes of his client and provided an exterior to enclose the preordained floor plan. Those internal arrangements, however, had little to do with the Smithsonian
Institution envisioned by Joseph Henry. When Owen lost his seat
in Congress and thus his seat on the Board of Regents, Henry took
charge of the plans of the building. Although the exterior was completed as envisioned in the Owen-Renwick plan, Henry succeeded
in altering the function or form of nearly every room in the edifice.

Ultimately Joseph Henry's castle was his home, but it was also
his prison. From 1855 to his death in 1878 Henry and his family
lived in the Castle, but he never ceased to hope that he could sell or
lease the building to the government for a United States National
Museum and move into smaller, less expensive quarters where his

Smithsonian could promote scientific research. The Castle, however, gave a physical, spatial, even a symbolic definition to the Smithsonian from which Henry was never to escape.

Without the Castle, Joseph Henry would have been able to fashion the Smithsonian into the clearinghouse of scientific research which he had always wished it to be. Robert Dale Owen, by insisting that the Castle be built, insured that the Smithsonian would continue to be what he had formulated in his legislative proposal: a multifunctional cultural institution, with art galleries, museums, libraries, and scientific research facilities all dedicated to the increase and diffusion of knowledge. That is, the Smithsonian as we know it today.

Chapter One

INCREASE AND DIFFUSION

L ONG before the United States Congress decided what the functions of the Smithsonian Institution were to be, architects and
politicians alike devoted a great deal of attention to what form the
Smithsonian Building was to take. James Smithson, a British chem-
ist, had left over half a million dollars for the founding of an institution at Washington for the "increase and diffusion of knowledge."
Such general terms led to differing interpretations of how the bequest might be carried out. Unfortunately, most of the men holding
those differing interpretations were members of the United States
Congress. The lack of a consensus on the part of those who cared
and a lack of interest on the part of everyone else delayed the establishment of the institution for the better part of eight years. Thus
there was ample time to debate the merits of various methods for
increasing and diffusing knowledge. During this extended gestation
period, two of the most prominent architects in America proposed
dramatically different conceptions of what a Smithsonian Building
should look like.

Although James Smithson had died in 1829, the United States
did not receive clear title to the money until 1835, when Smithson's
only nephew died childless. Congress authorized the Philadelphia
lawyer Richard Rush to travel to London to claim the bequest. Having served as attorney general, secretary of the Treasury, and United
States minister to the Court of St. James, Rush was peculiarly qualified to cope with the British bureaucracy; he succeeded in dislodg-
ing the funds in less than two years. Rush sailed for America in

possession of Smithson's personal belongings and the bequest in gold
bricks.[1]

In 1840, two years after the return of Rush, Alexander Jackson
Davis, a leading American architect of the Romantic era, drew up
plans for a Smithsonian Building. Davis had been the partner of
Ithiel Town from 1829 to 1835, and their commissions had included state capitols for Indiana and North Carolina, the United
States Customs House in New York City, the building for the
newly founded University of the City of New York—now New York
University—and numerous residences, churches, and commercial
buildings. In the mid-1830s Davis had formulated a series of three
plans for a new Patent Office Building for Washington. Robert Mills
was eventually chosen to modify and execute the designs of William
P. Elliot, a government clerk and former local agent for Town and
Davis; nevertheless, Davis was able to adapt the third and largest
project for the Patent Office to his Smithsonian design.[2]

Far more grand in scale than any previous public building in
America, the third Patent Office project (fig. 1) was to have been an
E-shaped edifice, seven hundred feet long, which would have made
it double the original length of the United States Capitol. The neoclassical building blended Greek and Roman elements with modern
innovations. Each prong of the E was to feature a Greek portico,
with the central portico leading inside to a rotunda beneath a low
Roman dome. At the rear of the building, another portico led to
the rotunda, and near each corner was a semicircular projection with
a colonnade. Davis allowed for almost no planar surfaces on the
exterior of the building; instead, load-bearing square piers alter-
nated with dramatically large windows. These "pilastrades," which
Town and Davis had used on the Customs House in New York and
on other neoclassical buildings, retained the rhythm of the columns
in the portico, maximized light, and minimized cost.

All of these features appeared in Davis's Smithsonian Building as
well, though the individual elements were rearranged and the whole
scaled down (fig. 2). Ten bays were cut from the length of the building, and the great central rotunda was replaced by two smaller ones
at each end of the museum. Davis pushed the outer wings into an I
shape so that the central portico dominated the composition. Since
the wings now projected equally to the front and rear, the two semicircular porches moved from the rear to the sides of the building,

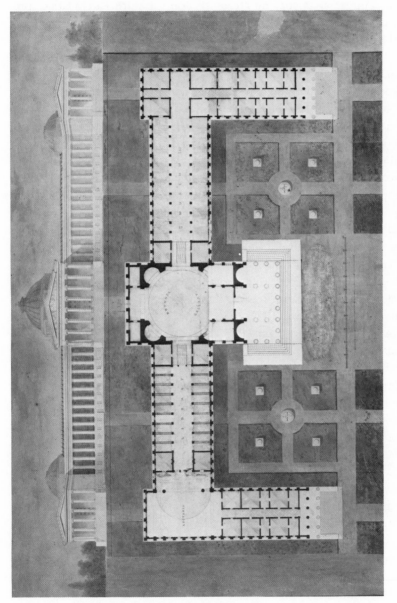

Figure 1. *Alexander Jackson Davis, Third Project for a Patent Office, Washington, D.C. 1834.*

3

opening off the two smaller rotundas. Where the rear portico had
stood, Davis placed an "Audience Hall," semicircular in plan and
surrounded by a curving arcade. As on the third Patent Office project, each wall was actually a pilastrade keeping up the rhythm of
the portico.[3]

That Davis would choose the neoclassical mode was hardly sur-
prising, although Town and Davis—with James H. Dakin, their
partner for a year and a half—had designed the building for New
York University in the Gothic mode. The public buildings of Washington were either late Palladian, such as the President's House, or
neoclassical, such as Mills's Treasury Building. An institution for
the increase and diffusion of knowledge, to be administered by the
federal government, could quite logically be housed in a similarly
styled building. Moreover, the Patent Office itself was an appropriate precedent for Davis, as it displayed patent models, the booty
of government expeditions, and even painting and sculpture. This
museum of the useful and fine arts could have easily served as a
symbol for the cultural aspirations of the young nation.[4]

Other neoclassical prototypes lay across the sea. The British Museum, by Sir Robert Smirke, was begun in 1823, although it was
not completed until 1847, and William Wilkins built the National
Gallery in London from 1833 to 1838. These two buildings summarized some seventy-five years of English fascination with Greek
culture, and firmly established the Greek mode as appropriate for
museums and galleries. An even more direct source of inspiration
for Davis may have been William Wilkins's University College,
London, built from 1826 to 1830, an E-shaped structure with Greek
portico and a dome—somewhat higher than the one Davis projected. Semicircular lecture halls curved out from the façade, similar
to the apsidal projections on both the third Patent Office and Smithsonian Building projects. Unlike the Davis schemes, University
College featured a rusticated base, and instead of Davis's pilastrade,
ornamental pilasters were attached to the walls. Nevertheless, the
work of Wilkins and Smirke provided Davis a stylistic precedent if
not specific inspiration.[5]

The sophistication of the Davis design could not, however, com-
pensate for the lack of political allies to sponsor his plan. Robert
Mills, who had emerged as the architect in charge of constructing

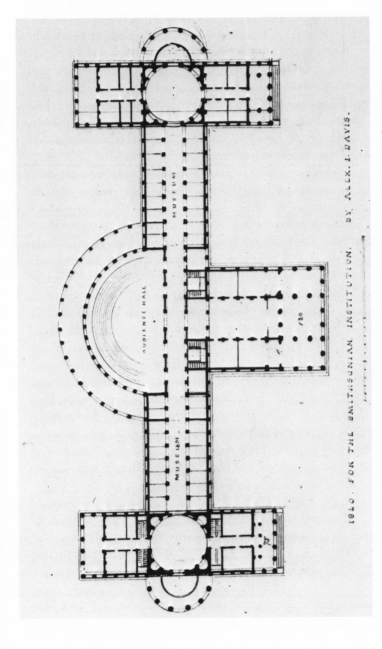

Figure 2. *Alexander Jackson Davis, Proposed Smithsonian Building. Ground plan, main floor. 1840.*

5

the Patent Office, paid much closer attention to the political exigencies of public architecture. William P. Elliot, whose plans Mills was adapting, bitterly complained that because Mills had rebuilt President Andrew Jackson's Tennessee home, the Hermitage, he was the greatest architect in the United States "in the eyes of the Old Hero." In addition to supervision of the Patent Office, Mills watched over the construction of the Treasury Building and the Post Office, both of his own design. By 1840, the east wing of the Treasury Building and the south wing of the Patent Office were finished, and Mills began to look out for new public projects. At this time a private organization, the National Institute for the Promotion of Science, was seeking to adapt to its own uses the Smithsonian bequest, upon which the Congress had delayed action for two years, and Mills joined forces with them to produce a project for a Smithsonian / National Institute Building (fig. 3).[6]

The National Institute for the Promotion of Science had been founded in May of 1840 at the home of Joel R. Poinsett, then secretary of war. Poinsett, a South Carolinian, had dabbled in Mexican politics and Mexican flowers while serving as American minister to that country; upon his expulsion by the Mexican government, he carried back to the United States the flower which would be called poinsettia. He had also organized the United States Exploring Expedition, commanded by Lieutenant Charles Wilkes, and Poinsett hoped that the fruits of that expedition would come under the care of the National Institute. Since a professionally executed plan for a National Institute Building might sufficiently impress the Congress with the competence and farsightedness of the group, and thus improve their chances of securing the Smithson bequest, Poinsett and the National Institute stood to benefit from an alliance with Robert Mills.[7]

Mills, like Poinsett a South Carolinian, had worked and studied under several important architects, first James Hoban, designer of the President's House in Washington, then Thomas Jefferson, and finally Benjamin Henry Latrobe. Like Latrobe, Mills was for the most part a neoclassicist, but willing to design in other modes when appropriate. Latrobe had built the first American residence in the Gothic mode, the Crammond House near Philadelphia, in 1799, and Mills had overseen the construction of Latrobe's Gothic mode

Bank of Philadelphia in 1807–1808. During that time, Latrobe presented Mills with the first two volumes of John Britton's *Architectural Antiquities of Great Britain*, which, years later, Mills would list as among the "principal works" to be consulted on the Norman style, along with "the Archeologia, Carter's Ancient Architecture of England . . . and Delaney's English Architecture."[8]

For the National Institute, Mills decided to draw upon the styles of the Middle Ages for inspiration. The "Saxon style," he believed, was associated "with great literary institutions" of Smithson's mother country. The great English literary institutions of the Middle Ages were, of course, Oxford and Cambridge, and in 1833 James H. Dakin had used the Chapel at King's College, Cambridge, as a source for Town, Davis and Dakin's New York University. In 1839 Mills

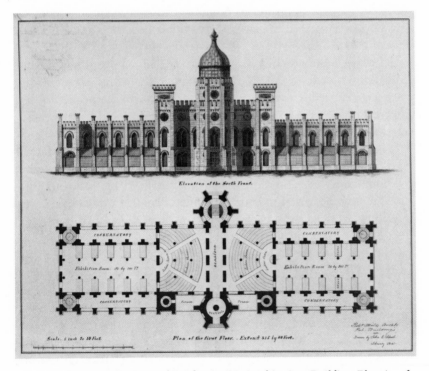

Figure 3. Robert Mills, Proposed Smithsonian/National Institute Building. Elevation of the south front and plan of the first floor. Dated February 1841.

himself had designed and built the Washington Jail, which included such medieval features as battlements and buttresses. Thus there were precedents for medieval styles in public buildings and institutions for the increase and diffusion of knowledge.[9]

The Smithsonian / National Institute Building was to have featured battlemented towers and parapets, with a three-story central section flanked on each side by two-story wings. In the middle of both the north and south façades were large octagonal towers culminating in onion-shaped domes. Entrance was through the base of the southern tower, and the main north tower and two square towers on the southern corners of the central section contained stairways. Two lecture rooms occupied the first floor of the main building, and on each side of these were the wings with their exhibition rooms.[10]

Both wings were supported by one-story flying buttresses, which were "introduced opposite the points of thrust of the groin arches"[11] inside. Mills planned to insert walls of glass between the buttresses, creating four conservatories. In plan and elevation, the Mills design was balanced and completely symmetrical. So too was Town, Davis and Dakin's New York University, although the wings of that structure were carried up a full three stories. The combination of a taller central section and the towers gave Mills's design much more of a vertical emphasis than at NYU.

The victory of William Henry Harrison over President Martin Van Buren in 1840 jeopardized the plans of both Mills and the National Institute, for Poinsett, displaced from his cabinet position, removed himself to South Carolina. The Institute thus lost its president, who had also been its most influential member. Poinsett's successors carried on in the attempt to become heirs of the Smithsonian bequest, but they were beset by their own mismanagement of the Wilkes expedition curiosities entrusted to them, and by political enemies in high places.[12]

The most potent congressional foe of the Institute was Senator Benjamin Tappan of Ohio, who was, like Poinsett, a Democrat, but a western Jacksonian Democrat. Tappan had the means to make his opposition felt as the chairman of the Joint Committee on the Library. Dealing with a grab bag of bills and petitions ranging from requests that the government buy Thomas Jefferson's papers or George

Catlin paintings to Alexandre Vattemare's scheme for an international exchange of scholarly research, the library committee was the receptacle of any proposals relating to education, research, or the fine arts. Senator Tappan was able to keep the National Institute's partisans at bay while he sought to overcome the other factions in the Senate and pass his own version of the Smithsonian Institution.[13]

The seemingly interminable delay on the Smithson bequest was beginning to reach scandalous lengths, and in 1842, four years after his return from England, Richard Rush mournfully wrote to Francis Markoe, a National Institute founder, comparing the inaction of the Congress to the case of the Girard trust in Rush's native Philadelphia. Girard, a banker, had provided in his will for an orphans' college, to be housed in a simple building with little ornamentation, and stipulated that no sectarian preacher be allowed inside the school's walls. Nicholas Biddle challenged the former provision, and Daniel Webster the latter. Biddle successfully demanded and built an enormously expensive but impressive Corinthian-colonnaded Greek temple for the school (fig. 4)—and Webster fought all the way to the Supreme Court only to have the Court declare that a deist's skepticism about God did not invalidate his will. Biddle's building had a more direct effect on the delay in the school's opening, since a legalistic interpretation of the will prevented the holding of classes until the buildings were completely finished, and the buildings were delayed by a lack of money on several occasions in separate years. The example of Girard College would later weigh heavily upon the minds of those involved with the Smithsonian.[14]

Senator Tappan, like other Jacksonians, was suspicious about incorporating *anything*, especially banks, but he overcame such antipathies long enough to offer—in December 1844—a bill to establish the Smithsonian Institution. The bill called for a museum with cabinets for the display of specimens from natural history, geology, and mineralogy; a library; a chemical laboratory; and a lecture room. The Tappan measure also provided for professors of natural history, chemistry, geology, and astronomy, but the thrust of the bill was towards popular lectures and experiments germane to the "productive and liberal arts of life, improvements in agriculture, in manufacture, in trades, and in domestic economy." Professors would be

Figure 4. Thomas U. Walter, Girard College, Philadelphia. 1833–1848.

funded so that they could provide useful information to the common man.[15]

Senator Rufus Choate (fig. 5), a Massachusetts Whig, spoke first against the bill when it reached the floor in January 1845. Choate asked his colleagues how Tappan's measure would increase and diffuse knowledge among men. "It proposes to do so," Choate said, "by establishing in this city a school or college for the purpose of instructing its pupils in the application of certain physical sciences to certain arts of life. The plan, if adopted, founds a college in Washington to teach the scientific principles of certain useful arts. That is the whole of it." To the modern ear Choate's criticism may seem less than damning, but in the United States Senate in 1845 "school or college" was a phrase with very specific connotations.

*Figure 5. Rufus Choate, Senator from Massachusetts
and later a Smithsonian Regent.*

John Quincy Adams had proposed a national university during his
term as president, but he failed to secure passage of the legislation.
In 1839, Senator Asher Robbins of Rhode Island had moved that
the Smithson bequest be used for a national university, but his bill
was tabled. Congress feared that a national university would turn
out to be a glorified local university, and disapproved of the idea of
the federal government's involving itself in an area traditionally left
to the states and private institutions. So Choate was actually playing
off the deep antipathy of his colleagues in his speech.[16]

A far more productive solution, Choate suggested, was the establishment of a great public library. Choate and George Perkins Marsh,
his leading ally in the House, were less concerned about providing
practical hints for the common man than they were about America's

standing in arts and letters vis-à-vis Europe. Marsh had proclaimed in a discourse delivered at Middlebury College that the nation which had already produced Washington Allston, Horatio Greenough, and George Bancroft could "reasonably hope that when our material facilities for advancement in knowledge and in taste shall be raised more nearly to the level of those of the more favoured of European countries, the works of our authors and our artists will rival the proudest labors . . . which ancient or modern times have produced." Excellence in academic, artistic, and literary endeavors, Choate and Marsh argued, depended upon the resources of a superior library.[17]

The alliance of Choate and Marsh was already some thirty years old. They had attended Dartmouth College together in the frenzied days of the attempted takeover of the college by the state. Choate, as librarian of his fraternity, had been arrested for attempting to fend off members of the university faction who wished to forcibly check out all the books, having already seized all the college-owned books. Not deterred by his criminal record for bibliophilia, Choate went on to build a private collection which held over two thousand volumes worth $40,000. Marsh also built up a substantial library, but more important for the Smithsonian, the alliance between the two men which began at Dartmouth and continued in the Congress would later extend to the Board of Regents of the Smithsonian.[18]

Choate was able to force Tappan's bill back into committee, and it emerged with a proviso that "an annual expenditure of not less than $20,000 out of the interest of the fund is authorized to be made in the purchase of books and manuscripts for the library of the institution. . . ." The amended bill also provided for the employment of a librarian and assistants. Having met the requirements of the library faction, the bill passed the Senate in January of 1845.[19]

As the measure advanced to the House of Representatives, yet another congressman began to take interest in the Smithsonian bequest: Robert Dale Owen, a first-term Democrat from Indiana. Robert Dale Owen was the son of the utopian socialist Robert Owen. Born in Glasgow, Scotland, in 1801, the younger Owen attended, from 1818 to 1821, an experimental school run by Philip Emanuel Fellenberg on his estate, Hofwyl, near Berne, Switzerland. Hofwyl actually consisted of two schools, a "Literary Institution" for the sons of the upper classes and an "Agricultural Institution" for orphans and the sons of peasants. The faculty of the Literary Institution, Owen later recalled, imbued him with "three years of German thought and German study." In his youth Owen had eagerly read the works of Sir Walter Scott, but after three years at Hofwyl his favorites had become Schiller and Goethe. The Nibelungenlied, "the Iliad of Germany," as Owen called it, was also a "favorite text-book at Hofwyl." He was able to apply the lessons of the Agricultural Institution as well, for, on his return from Switzerland to Scotland, Owen found himself "occupied, for several years, in the personal supervision of the village schools" at his father's model industrial community, New Lanark.[20]

Robert Dale Owen came to America in 1825, when his father purchased the buildings and town of Harmony, Indiana, from George Rapp, the pastor of a group of German Lutheran schismatics. The elder Owen rechristened it New Harmony, and retained an English architect, Stedman Whitwell, to draw up plans for the community. He responded with a scheme reminiscent of the utopian industrial cities envisioned by Claude Nicolas Ledoux earlier in the century. The pyramids, cubes, spheres, and other idealized geometric forms of Ledoux's elaborate projects gave way to a medieval-like quadrangle, with public buildings at the four corners and at the midpoint of each outer wall (fig. 6). Interspersed among the public buildings were ranges of dwellings, signified by rows of high-pitched gables. The whole was to be "raised above the level of the natural surface, and surrounded by an esplanade," and the internal courtyard featured botanical gardens and exercise grounds. So grand was the scheme that it was never built; George Rapp's original buildings were the only ones the utopians could afford.[21]

The communal phase of New Harmony lasted less than two years, but even after Robert Dale Owen acknowledged the failure of the project, he resolved to stay in America. He became an editor and activist in New York, advocating free thought and championing radical causes. In time, though, Owen rejoined his family in New Harmony, and after a few years of attempting to take care of family business, was elected to the Indiana State Assembly. As a politician, Owen was not a crowd-pleaser, but he was a man of great optimism and greater determination, and in 1843 he was elected to the United

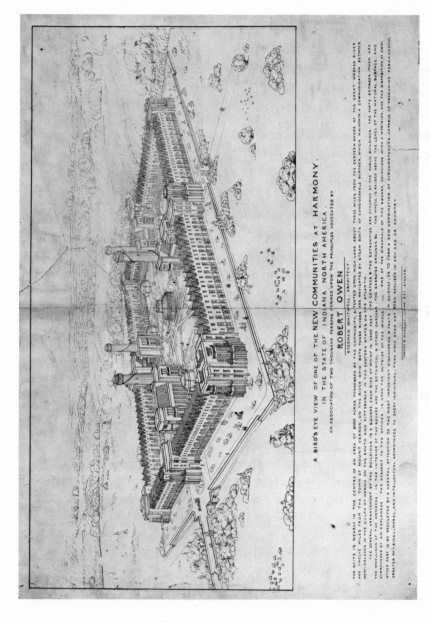

Figure 6. Robert Owen and Stedman Whitwell, Proposed community. New Harmony, Indiana. 1825.

States Congress. For the first two years of his stay in Washington, Owen roomed at the same boarding house as his fellow western Democrat Benjamin Tappan.[22]

Shortly after the Senate passed their compromise Smithsonian bill, both Rufus Choate and Benjamin Tappan left the Congress. The action now shifted to the House, where, on three separate occasions, John Quincy Adams had futilely attempted to apply Smithson's money toward a great observatory modeled after that at Greenwich. Robert Dale Owen, in December 1845, introduced his own substitute Smithsonian bill, the features of which distinctly echoed those of Tappan's bill. Expenditures on books for the library were not to exceed $5,000 annually (as opposed to $20,000 in the Choate-Tappan compromise), and provision was made for a chemical laboratory, halls for cabinets of natural history, including a geological and mineralogical cabinet, a professor of agriculture, horticulture, and rural economy and an assistant, and a normal school, which was Owen's major innovation.[23]

A select committee on the Smithsonian bequest took up consideration of the bill. Owen, as chairman, spent much of his time warding off the efforts of John Quincy Adams to eliminate the normal school. The chairman was able to thwart Adams, but another member of the committee, George Perkins Marsh, succeeded in doubling the appropriation for the library to $10,000, though that fell far short of the $20,000 which his friend Choate had been able to extract from Tappan. Jefferson Davis laid low, though no doubt he watched carefully after the interests of his close friend Alexander Dallas Bache, superintendent of the United States Coast Survey. The committee reported out a compromise bill in late February 1846. Debate began on April twenty-second.[24]

Robert Dale Owen led off in support of the bill, immediately alluding to the waste of the Girard trust. Of that noble fund, he said, three quarters of a million dollars were spent without one child's having reaped the benefits intended by the donor. A magnificent Greek temple, which outshines even the Parthenon, had arisen, but the will of the founder had been thwarted. Yet, Owen insisted, the House could not throw stones at the city of Philadelphia, while the Smithsonian bequest remained under the consideration of the Congress.[25]

As to the relative merits of a library and a normal school, Owen remained convinced that the latter would most effectively increase and diffuse knowledge. The Library of Congress, he pointed out, was already a great national library. Further, Owen wondered whether there were "a hundred thousand volumes in the world worth reading? I doubt it much." Normal schools, on the other hand, would spread teachers across the land, and increase the general level of knowledge. He recommended to the House the report of Alexander Dallas Bache on European normal schools, done while Bache was the president of Girard College. The Smithson bequest must be used, Owen concluded, "to reach the minds and hearts of the masses; we must diffuse knowledge *among men*. . . ."

George Perkins Marsh vigorously attacked the notion of professors disseminating practical information. A laboratory, he claimed, "is a charnel house . . . and experiments are but the dry bones of science." Marsh had praise for the natural sciences a few sentences later, especially since some branches of science could greatly benefit from a large library. Marsh did speak well of the compromise, though, and alluded to the recently concluded debate on the Oregon boundary dispute between Great Britain and the United States, which had given rise to the slogan "Fifty-four Forty or Fight!" However great the differences on the Smithsonian issue seem to be, Marsh said, "we shall probably find ourselves in the end obliged to settle down on the parallel of 49°." No one on the committee that drafted it believed it to be the best bill, Marsh asserted, but it did succeed in harmonizing discordant views.[26]

The amendment process demonstrated the strength of the library faction. The expenditure on the library was increased from $10,000 to $25,000, higher even than the concession Tappan had made to Choate. To pay for the massive library, the normal school was eliminated, as was the series of popular lectures and popular publications, the professorships, and the horticultural experiments. The final form of the bill, drafted by William Jervis Hough of New York, placed the Institution on the block just east of the Patent Office, subject to the objection of the president or his cabinet. By placing the building on an urban block rather than on the Mall, the bill reinforced the congressional disavowal of agricultural experiments.[27]

The final draft of the Smithsonian bill succeeded in garnering a majority, but a clear-cut division of ranks existed on the vote. The rift was not partisan, but sectional. Of forty-two congressmen from the deep South present for the vote, all but six voted against the bill. Among those in favor were Henry Hilliard of Alabama and Jefferson Davis of Mississippi, both eventually to become Smithsonian Regents. In the northern states, the bill passed 48–13, while in the border and western states the margin of passage was a narrow 31–26. Evidently the South saw in the Smithsonian bill a dangerous extension of federal powers and an expensive outlay of federal funds. It was what John Quincy Adams had assailed in his diary a few months before as the mentality of John C. Calhoun: "it will be persisted in by the South Carolina school of politics and morals to the last, without any idea of returning the money, but with the purpose of defeating any useful application of it." The close vote and the ominous rift indicated that there was a stronghold of future opposition in the House.[28]

Robert Dale Owen, however, seemed optimistic about further influencing the nascent Institution. The compromise bill had solved the dilemma of what "increase and diffusion" meant by allocating something for each faction. The direction the Institution would take rested in the hands of the Institution's Board of Regents. Owen had been appointed one of the regents from the House of Representatives, along with William Jervis Hough, the New York lawyer responsible for the final draft of the bill, and Henry Hilliard, one of the six congressmen from the deep South to vote in favor of the bill. The Senate was to be represented by Sidney Breese of Illinois, Isaac Pennybacker of Virginia, and George Evans of Maine. The more powerful figures on the Board of Regents came from the private citizens appointed. Rufus Choate, retired from the Senate, would never retire from promoting libraries public and private. Alexander Dallas Bache, superintendent of the United States Coast Survey, possessed formidable credentials as a scientist and almost as formidable allies in the halls of power. Colonel Joseph G. Totten, with Bache a member of the National Institute, was the chief of the Army Corps of Engineers. Also on the Board of Regents were Richard Rush, who had retrieved the Smithson money from Britain; William Campbell Preston, the president of South Carolina College, the present University of South Carolina, and a former senator; and Gideon Hawley, a distinguished educator from New York State. Chief Justice Roger B. Taney and Vice-President George M. Dallas were regents *ex officio*, as was Mayor William Winston Seaton of Washington, a venerated and powerful figure.[29]

Owen had already seized upon a loophole in the law's dictation of a building site. He wrote to Richard Rush on August 16 that the amendment had been "hastily and inconsiderately adopted," and that he had already spoken to the president, his cabinet, and the commissioner of patents. They "all agree in refusing their assent to any such absurd arrangement" which would cut off the Institution from "all ground for agricultural experiments, or even a botanical garden." The placement of the building near the Patent Office would have an important effect on the development of the Institution, and Owen was quick to challenge it. He also anticipated that the first session of the Board of Regents would determine much about the Institution and its building. To Rush he wrote: "We shall have to select the location, and to make some preparations, I suppose, for the buildings. Upon judicious action on both these points much of the future character and utility of the Institution may depend." Owen's casual reference to "some preparations, I suppose, for the buildings" was quite carefully modulated to imply that he was interested in the question of the building but not overly eager. In fact, Owen had been engaged in the preparation of plans for the Smithsonian Building for over a year, in conjunction with his brother, David Dale Owen, and with Robert Mills.[30]

In the summer of 1845, after passage of the Senate Choate-Tappan compromise, but months before the opening of the session during which the Institution would finally be established, Congressman Owen began to correspond with David Dale Owen and Robert Mills. Robert Dale encouraged his brother to draw up his own plans, expressing confidence that David Dale would "consult utility first, in the various internal arrangements, and let architectural elegance follow, as a secondary" consideration. A general trading of plans between the Owen brothers and Mills took place, with Mills sending a "rough sketch" of his 1841 plan to New Harmony, and seeking out his old drawings from Joel R. Poinsett in South Carolina, and from the new secretary of war, William P. Marcy, whose "diligent search" turned up nothing.[31]

Robert Dale Owen approved of Mills's selection of the "Anglo-Saxon style," which, Owen was confident, was "solid, imposing, and probably the most economical among ornamental styles." David

Dale Owens agreed, writing his brother that the "Norman style" was the most economical, "and best admits the introduction of all sorts of conveniences. It recommends itself, also, for Public Buildings, on account of its simplicity and massiveness of structure." Phrases like "simplicity" and "massiveness" had formerly been applied to the neoclassical mode, but the Owen brothers sought to adapt them to the medieval mode, even if the Norman seemed simple only in contrast to the Gothic.[32]

The Owen brothers also agreed with Mills's evaluation of the associational content of the medieval mode. "Considering," wrote David Dale Owen, "the country which gave birth to and cherished the donor of the bequest, and that our country affords, as yet, few examples of this oldest English manner, it strikes me that the selection of this style for the Smithsonian Institution is particularly judicious." The association of the medieval styles with England was strengthened in the 1830s and 1840s by the construction of the new House of Parliament, London, by Sir Charles Barry and A. W. N. Pugin, especially since Pugin was given to claiming that the Gothic was the English national style.[33]

Although David Dale Owen had access to the earlier Mills design, his own plan departed from that of Mills in a number of ways. Whereas Mills's entire building, including conservatories, was 315 feet by 80, the central block alone of David Dale Owen's plan was 237 by 46 on the interior. He then placed wings to the east and west, connected to the main building by ranges. On the north side of the ranges, "cloisters or piazzas" provided a covered walkway between the wings and the main building, and on the south conservatories extended twenty feet beyond the line of the main building.[34]

Owen converted Mills's octagonal tower in the center of the south façade to a larger square tower, which would hold rooms, including a room for the regents, as well as stairs. On the north, he retained the central octagonal tower, but transformed its ground floor into a porte cochere with rounded arches large enough for a carriage to pass through. Smaller octagonal towers were to grace the four corners of the main building. Those on the north would contain spiral staircases, those on the south manually operated elevators for freight.

The main building was to be three stories tall. The first floor would hold the principal lecture room and library, as well as a smaller library room. The second floor was reserved exclusively for a mu-

seum, with cases placed between windows to create a series of alcoves. Galleries were to encircle the room at the level of the middle
bar of the windows, and another row of cases was to run down the
center of the room. The third floor was to contain two more lecture
rooms, one for scientific demonstrations, the other for the agricultural department. The wings provided yet another two lecture rooms,
for chemistry on the east and art on the west.

Each lecture room thus had a specific function—even the principal lecture room, in addition to serving as a general assembly hall,
"might be occupied by the professor of common school instruction."
In his original manuscript, Owen had written "Normal," but then
crossed it out and inserted "common school." His brother's bill had
a provision for a normal school, but David Dale Owen apparently
saw a common school as a possible alternative.

David Dale Owen was quite aware of the difficulties experienced
by men of science in using facilities designed by architects. He referred to *Travels in North America*, by the British geologist Charles
Lyell, for examples such as Girard College in Philadelphia and University College, London, by William Wilkins. Of the latter, Lyell
recalled that when "the professor of chemistry enquired for the
chimney of his laboratory, he was informed that there was none, and
to remove the defect, a flue was run up which encroached upon a
handsome staircase, and destroyed the symmetry of the architect's
design." Owen pointed to the room in the east range, where students in chemistry could "engage in practical experiments and analysis." This, he wrote, had been an important addition to the laboratories of Justus "Liebig and most of the celebrated European
chemists."

The style of architecture was not, Owen claimed, the "earliest
and strictest form" of the Norman, which he defined as using exclusively rounded arches, but rather as it appeared toward the end of
the twelfth century, when pointed arches were occasionally used.
He assumed that the appearance of rounded and pointed arches together meant that medieval designers had planned their simultane-
ous use. This view would not be borne out by later research, however. Actually pointed arches were added only when rounded arches
went out of style while a building was long under construction.
Nevertheless, Owen was encouraged by what he saw as a precedent
for eclecticism.

As for materials, Owen proposed, "for the sake of economy," that the building should be constructed of brick, and then painted the color of stone. He suggested, however, that the "finishing of doors and windows, also the conservatory front, the pilasters and arches of the cloister and the other ornamental details" should be of cast iron. The first half of the nineteenth century had seen an increasing use of cast iron for bridges, conservatories, and railroad sheds, as well as for interiors such as that of the Bibliothèque Sainte Geneviève in Paris, by Henri Labrouste, which was under construction as Owen wrote. His proposal for the Smithsonian Building anticipated the great popularity of cast iron architecture in America, which would climax in the 1850s with the cast-iron store fronts of James Bogardus of New York.[35]

Robert Dale Owen's provision for a normal school had been struck from the final bill, but his brother's plans were to be most influential, since the competitors for the Smithsonian Building were given copies of David Dale Owen's plans, along with certain letters between the Owen brothers on the subject of the building. Almost all of the competitors were to base their own floor plans on the one drawn up in New Harmony.

Thus, Robert Dale Owen's letter to Richard Rush with its casual reference to "some preparations, I suppose, for the buildings"[36] can be read as an attempt, without the appearance of zeal, to place Rush in a building frame of mind. It was, perhaps, the last time that Robert Dale Owen would show restraint in advocating his plans for the Smithsonian Building.

Chapter Two

THE BUSINESS OF AN ARCHITECT

A LTHOUGH the Board of Regents of the Smithsonian Institution first met in September 1846, they did not choose their chief executive officer until almost three months later. In the meantime, Alexander Dallas Bache, Rufus Choate, and Robert Dale Owen emerged as the three most influential regents. Owen threw himself into the business of finding an architect, and by the end of November he had in mind not only an architect but also a specific design. As in his letter to Richard Rush, Owen attempted to predispose the other regents toward his favored plan, but his unabashed advocacy of that plan in advance of the official deadline for competition entries would eventually engender confusion and animosity on the part of the other competing architects.

On a hot September day, unusually warm even for Washington, the Board of Regents gathered in the Post Office Building at Eighth and E Streets, N.W., for their first meeting. Business was taken care of quickly. Vice-President George M. Dallas was elected interim president of the board and Representative William Jervis Hough became the interim secretary. After determining to meet the next morning in the neighboring Patent Office, they adjourned, but politicking went on before and after the meeting. Senator Isaac Pennybacker of Virginia had called on President James K. Polk that morning, and two others, Vice-President Dallas and Richard Rush, spent an hour at the White House that evening.[1]

The regents as a whole were an extremely well-connected group.

*Figure 7. General Joseph G. Totten, United States Army Corps
of Engineers.*

Perhaps the most well-connected with the world of politics and the
world of science—and with each other—were Colonel Joseph G.
Totten and Alexander Dallas Bache. Totten and Bache filled the two
places on the Board of Regents which had been reserved for members of the National Institute residing in Washington. But the two
had known each other long before the National Institute had come
into existence.

Joseph G. Totten (fig. 7), born in New Haven in 1788, had been
raised by his uncle and guardian, Jared Mansfield. When Mansfield

was named professor of mathematics at the newly formed United States Military Academy, his ward entered as a cadet. Totten became the tenth graduate of West Point, and was immediately assigned as secretary to the surveyor general of the Northwestern Territory, better known to Totten as "Uncle Jared." From 1808 to 1838 Totten served as an engineer on harbor and coast defense, and on river and harbor improvements. He continued to maintain his West Point connections, especially with Sylvanus Thayer, superintendent at the Point from 1817 to 1833, and Professor Dennis Hart Mahan. In 1838, Totten was promoted to colonel, made chief of the Army Corps of Engineers and inspector of the Military Academy. Two years later, he was one of eight men who gathered in the home of Joel R. Poinsett in Washington to found the National Institute. His appointment as a Smithsonian regent came just as he turned fifty-eight.[2]

At forty, Alexander Dallas Bache (fig. 8) was the youngest regent, but both his looks and his credentials belied it. Bache had been the youngest cadet all four of his years at West Point and had finished first in the class each year. After serving the year after his graduation as assistant to Professor of Engineering Dennis Hart Mahan, Bache was assigned to the construction of Fort Adams in Newport, Rhode Island, where his commanding officer was Major Joseph G. Totten. Two years later, Lieutenant Bache, then twenty-two, resigned his commission to become professor of natural philosophy and chemistry at the University of Pennsylvania. On July 19, 1836—Bache's thirtieth birthday—he was unanimously elected president of Girard College. Bache then spent some two years in Europe, examining the educational systems and collecting scientific apparatus and fine wines. While in Europe, he sometimes traveled with his close friend and fellow American scientist Joseph Henry of the College of New Jersey—now Princeton—and also met the young Philadelphia architect of the proposed Girard College, Thomas U. Walter. Back in America, Bache hoped to open the school in the fall of 1838, but Philadelphia politics continued to delay the opening by the insistence that Biddle and Walter's Greek Temple should be completely finished first. Bache turned his attention to a reorganization of the Philadelphia public schools, and eventually resigned the presidency of Girard College to return to the University of Pennsylvania. A

Figure 8. Alexander Dallas Bache, Superintendent, United States Coast Survey.

year later Bache was appointed superintendent of the United States Coast Survey, and he and his wife moved to Washington.[3]

Bache was able to complement his impressive personal record with a well-connected family tree. He bore the name of his maternal grandfather, Alexander J. Dallas, Madison's secretary of the Treasury, and Vice-President George M. Dallas was his uncle. Above all hovered the aura of his great-grandfather, Benjamin Franklin. Bache's brother-in-law was Senator Robert J. Walker of Mississippi, and Senator Jefferson Davis had been a close friend since their West Point days.[4]

Thus on that steamy September day in Washington, Bache saw his uncle George chosen interim president of the Institution, and on the next day Dallas was elected as the first chancellor of the Smithsonian. A few minutes later, Dallas named the Executive Committee: Robert Dale Owen, Joseph G. Totten, and William W. Seaton, with the latter serving as chairman. The chancellor also appointed Owen, Bache, and Henry Hilliard to the Committee on Organization, and Choate, Rush and Gideon Hawley to the Library Committee. Once again, visiting President Polk was the evening's entertainment. Senator George Evans of Maine and Rufus Choate paid their respects to the president, and Regents Rush and Pennybacker paid them again.[5]

The next day, September 9, 1846, the Regents assembled on the public grounds west of the Capitol and south of the White House, where they met President Polk at 9 A.M. Polk noted in his diary that he spent "nearly an hour with them on foot in examining the grounds [of the Mall]. Opinions were freely expressed." Polk sensed that most of the regents favored the location between Twelfth and Fourteenth Streets, and the president, too, thought it the "most eligible site." Opposition came from Mayor Seaton, who favored the area between Ninth and Twelfth Streets, closer to the Capitol grounds. This area, Polk thought, was much lower than the land to the west of it, "and in no sense, as it strikes me, so eligible." Polk was wary, moreover, of the economic interests which a mayor of Washington might attempt to advance. In his diary Polk recorded that he had heard from "private sources" that Mayor Seaton was much concerned with improving the area around the Centre Market. The president regretted that "any citizen of Washington was appointed a Regent. The Smithsonian Institute is a national Institution," Polk wrote, "and should be located and conducted without reference to individual or private interests."[6]

Whether Polk's sources were correct about the particulars, Seaton was probably concerned about the future of the Centre Market, which was on the south side of Pennsylvania Avenue at Seventh Street, and he was definitely concerned about the general economic impact which the Institution would make. In his annual report to the City Council, published in his own newspaper, the *National Intelligencer*, the mayor had suggested that since the decision to rebuild the Capitol after the War of 1812, "nothing has occurred calculated to exert so important an influence on the fortunes of this city, even unto the most distant future, as the founding of this great and annually growing institution. . . ." That Seaton remained as treasurer of the Institution long after his term as regent expired indicates the intensity of his belief in the favorable influence of the Smithsonian upon Washington.[7]

Also on the Mall that morning, mingling with the regents but unnoted in the president's diary or any official document, was Isaiah Rogers, the Boston architect responsible for two trend-setting hotels, the Tremont House in Boston and the Astor House in New York. He had arrived in Washington on Monday, September 7, and called upon Mayor Seaton and Rufus Choate—"He goes for a very large library," observed Rogers to his diary—and spoke briefly to Robert Dale Owen. The next evening Rogers paid another call on Owen, this time coming away with a copy of the plans by David Dale Owen, apparently to be used as an example of what the regents were looking for. As to the meeting on the Mall, Rogers noted only the "many views of the subject" and the inconclusiveness of the discussion.[8]

After an hour, the president returned to the White House and the regents to the Patent Office. Once there, Robert Dale Owen presented to the board the plans of his brother, along with the rendering by Robert Mills. A committee was then created "to take such measures as may be deemed by them most proper to obtain plans for the erection of buildings." The chancellor, the secretary, and the Executive Committee constituted the Committee on the Building: Dallas, Hough, Seaton, Owen, and Totten. The committee was to determine the best methods of warming, lighting, and ventilation, the best material for the exterior of the building, and the best site. The regents also authorized the committee to purchase relevant texts relating to "architecture, bibliography and the like" if necessary for the completion of their tasks.[9]

After the close of business of the full Board of Regents, the newly appointed building committee met with Isaiah Rogers. The architect "received instructions to procure and make a sketch of a plan" based on that of David Dale Owen, which Rogers could revise as he thought best. The committee, which was planning a tour of several cities on the east coast to discuss the building with prominent architects, made an appointment to see Rogers in Boston two weeks later, when they could tour the important buildings there together. [10]

A day or so after the regents dispersed, Alexander Dallas Bache received a letter from a friend and fellow scientist, James Renwick, Sr., of Columbia College in New York. Bache had tried to call on Renwick during his last trip to New York, and Renwick regretted that they had missed each other. But after a few brief comments about some magnetic observations, Renwick's letter came straight to the point. "Among the first things which will probably come up at the meeting of the Board of Regents of the Smithsonian Institution, of which I perceive you as a member, will be the question of an appropriate building. In case anything of that sort is spoken of may I ask you to bring the name of my son James to the notice of the Board?" Professor Renwick pointed to Grace Church in New York as exhibiting any talent which young James possessed as an architect and builder. "I may be partial," he wrote, "but I do not doubt that it is the handsomest church in the United States, as well as least costly in proportion to its size. . . . It seats more persons than Trinity Church, and while that has cost $370,000, Grace Church does not exceed $75,000." Renwick informed Bache that he had sent a letter to Colonel Totten dealing with the same subject in more detail, "particularly in reference to a contract, to the style of building and to the material." He had further suggested that Totten circulate the letter among the other Regents. It would most certainly have been called to the attention of Robert Dale Owen, who seemed to be the most enthusiastic member of the Building Committee. [11]

On September 14, Robert Dale Owen and William J. Hough left by train for Philadelphia, the first stop on their architectural tour of eastern cities. Colonel Totten, the third member of the subcommittee, could not join the party until they reached Boston. Both Philadelphia architects William Strickland and Thomas U. Walter were out of town, and word was left for Walter and perhaps for Strickland that the committee would see them after completing their business in New York and Boston. John Haviland was also away

from home; information was left with his son. That left John Notman, a Scottish-born architect then supervising the construction of
the Athenaeum. He was "seen and repeatedly conversed with." Owen,
Hough, and Notman visited Philadelphia buildings that varied in
style from the Greek to the Gothic and the Italianate. Strickland's
Second Bank of the United States—by then in use as a customs
house—had been the first American public building to be modeled
on the Parthenon, and Walter's Girard College promised to be the
most lavish application of the Greek mode to date. Haviland's Eastern State Penitentiary, just a few blocks from Girard College, offered
massiveness of another sort, sheer stone walls topped with medieval
battlements. In the older part of the city, Notman's Athenaeum
brought to town the refinement of the Italian Renaissance as dis-
tilled in England by Sir Charles Barry and William Wilkins. Notman also accompanied Owen and Hough to Trenton, New Jersey,
where they visited the State Lunatic Asylum and the renovated State
House. Owen's report to the regents noted Mr. Notman's "constant
presence and intelligent remarks." [12]

Tuesday evening, Owen and Hough caught the train to New York,
in order that Hough might make an early morning appointment to
examine a quarry. From Wednesday to Saturday they conferred with
Richard Upjohn, Owen G. Warren, Joseph Wells and his partner
David Arnot, and James Renwick, Jr., who was accompanied by his
father, Professor James Renwick. Owen and Hough visited John
Haviland's famous prison in the Egyptian mode, The Tombs, Richard Upjohn's Gothic masterpiece Trinity Church, and all three of
young Renwick's churches. Of the latter, Grace Church and Calvary
Church were Gothic, while the Church of the Puritans was in the
Norman or Romanesque style. [13]

Owen and Hough continued on to Boston, and checked into the
Tremont House. The hotel's architect, Isaiah Rogers, took the two
regents on an inspection tour of Faneuil Hall, the Customs House,
and other structures. Colonel Totten joined the group on Tuesday,
and they held further discussions with Rogers and with his fellow
New England architect Ammi B. Young. On September 23 they
left for Washington. Owen would consult with the Cincinnati architects Henry Walters and Howard Daniels on his way to New
Harmony, but already one architect stood out among the others for

Owen. He was James Renwick, Jr., the youngest of the architects the committee had seen, being six weeks shy of his twenty-eighth birthday.[14]

Renwick had achieved his status by a combination of family connections, financial clout, and an almost precocious flair for designing. Born in New York City in 1818, he was the son of Professor James Renwick and Margaret Anne Brevoort. The senior Renwick's marriage to Margaret, who was the daughter of an eccentric vegetable farmer, had "greatly mortified" his mother, for, noted Renwick's brother-in-law Charles Wilkes, "no two appeared to be so ill matched." Young James grew up in a household dominated by "a shrewd and, I might add, a tyrannical wife and mother of no pleasant address or manners." In the Wilkes family, "the usual expression was Poor Uncle James." In 1819, a year after young James was born, the family business, which James senior had attempted to run, failed, and Renwick was forced to declare bankruptcy. He accepted the position of professor of natural philosophy at Columbia College, and the family thenceforth lived on the campus in a Dickensian sort of genteel poverty. "There were many ridiculous things about them," noted Wilkes, "but a strict economy at all times."[15]

The senior Renwick, an authoritative consultant on many an engineering project, was "meekness itself" in family matters, and probably withdrew quite frequently into his avocation, water coloring. Young James could browse through his father's renderings, which may have been done while wandering through England and Scotland with Washington Irving. The imaginary itinerary on which young James could embark included Windsor Castle, Ludlow Castle, Warwick Castle, and Tintern Abbey. Thus while the elder Renwick would claim to have been "brought up in the school of Palladio," his son early discovered a world of pointed arches and battlements. Even the elder Renwick, despite his Palladian upbringing, had proposed a building in the Gothic for Columbia College in 1814.[16]

Young Renwick attended Columbia, where he was taught by his father. After his graduation in 1836, he worked for a brief time as a construction engineer on the Erie Railroad. Meanwhile, his father, who would eventually bring his sons Henry and Edward onto the payroll of the United States Boundary Commission, procured for James junior a position as second assistant for New York's Croton Aqueduct. The system had been designed by Professor David B.

Douglass, Professor Renwick's counterpart at the University of the City of New York, but in 1836 John B. Jervis, former head of the Delaware and Hudson Canal project, took over as chief engineer. Jervis knew the elder Renwick, who once, as consultant to the Delaware and Hudson Canal, had discovered an error in Jervis's calculations. In Renwick's report to the board, Jervis recalled, "excepting this error he found nothing to criticize, and as a whole spoke favorably of my report and expressed confidence in my ability to successfully conduct the work." For whatever reason he was hired, young Renwick worked his way up the staff, which, at the height of construction, employed some twenty men at the rank of second assistant or better, and when water gushed into the distributing reservoir at the outskirts of the city—Fifth Avenue and Fortieth Street—on July 4, 1842, it flowed into the first major structure built under the supervision of James Renwick, Jr. With its battered walls and massive corner pavillions, the distributing reservoir had an Egyptian feel to it, and even Horatio Greenough admired the structure, with its lack of applied ornament and its businesslike demeanor. [17]

In the meantime, young Renwick's maternal grandfather, Henry Brevoort, died. The Brevoort farm, strategically located at what is now Broadway and Tenth, was instantly transformed from a vegetable patch to a real estate bonanza. Philip Hone, the businessman and former Whig mayor of New York, estimated that the farm "which cost [Brevoort] a few hundred dollars . . . is now worth to his heirs half a million." The financial straits of the Renwick family were now over, but in one sense, the years of close living had affected young James. Observed his uncle, Charles Wilkes: "Of James there is little to be said; I do not think he is at all popular. . . . His general reputation is close and contracted in Money Matters and the same may be said of the youngest, Edward." George Templeton Strong, a classmate of Renwick's at Columbia, considered him to be "that most windy of all bags of conceit and coxcombry that ever dubbed themselves Architect. . . ." The "infatuated monkey," Strong raged to his diary, did not show the slightest trace or germ of feeling for his art, and was cut out by nature to be a boss carpenter. Renwick's "vanity and pretension," which Strong would find "endurable and excusable in an artist, are not to be endured in a mechanic, and especially not in one who is a mechanic in spite of his ennobling vocation, and degrades, vulgarizes and pollutes every glorious idea and form of the successive eras of Christian art that he travesties and tampers with, as a sacrifice to the stolidity of building committees and his own love of fat jobs and profitable contracts." Although Renwick was very much concerned with the "business of an architect," Strong's sympathies with the New York Ecclesiological Society, a group of high Episcopalians devoted to "pure" Gothic churches, suggests that he was offended by Renwick's free handling of elements from different medieval styles, and not just by his consciousness of money matters.[18]

The inheritance not only lifted the Renwicks out of financial stringency but also played a crucial role in young James's first bid for a building contract. In May 1843, Henry Brevoort, Jr., acting as representative, sold a parcel of the Brevoort estate to Grace Church, Episcopal, of which both Renwick senior and Brevoort junior had been vestrymen years before. By the last day of June, a number of plans had been submitted to the building committee. Two months later, the clerk of the vestry submitted the abstract of the title to the Brevoort property, and the building committee submitted the name of the winning architect: James Renwick, Jr., age twenty-five. The estimated cost of the church was $57,685.[19]

Grace Church was Renwick's first major commission, and a rather sophisticated design (fig. 9). Like Richard Upjohn's Trinity Church, Grace had a single front tower, but Renwick opted for a cross-shaped plan—Trinity had no transepts—and used extensive Gothic ornamentation. Though Renwick, like Upjohn, demonstrated a close familiarity with the writings of A. W. N. Pugin, Grace shows the influence of French as well as English Gothic. Though family connections had gotten him entree, young James came through with an impressive performance.[20]

On October 30, 1843, the cornerstone was laid, or, to be more precise, fell into place, "scattering the mortar in all directions over the clergy and laity without distinction." Trivial in itself, the incident foreshadowed other blunders in execution, on not only Grace Church but other Renwick buildings as well. Fourteen months later, Renwick fired his mason, Andrew Young, "for unworkmanlike execution of the work and other causes." A new contract was drawn up with A. O. Price, but that artisan "lost his life by the explosion of a bombshell" soon after. Delays in the construction gradually forced

Figure 9. James Renwick, Jr., Grace Church, New York. 1843. Photo from 1916.

the cost up to around $75,000, which was by no means a gross overrun. The church was finally consecrated on March 7, 1846.[21]

A shortage of funds forced Renwick to place a wooden steeple on top of the tower, causing the church to become widely known as "Renwick's toothpick," and rumors circulated that a wooden tower was erected because the foundation of the building could not support a steeple of marble. So prevalent and persistent were these rumors that in 1863 the surviving members of the Grace building committee published a letter insisting that the wooden steeple had been chosen as an economy measure. George Templeton Strong was more concerned with economy measures on the interior, particularly the use of plaster to cover the columns. After a minute inspection of the church while it was still under construction in 1845, Strong commented in his diary that "the pipe-cleaners of columns that support the clerestory will tend to impress the congregation with a sense of the uncertainty of human life and suggest profitable meditation on the instability of things temporal. It's positively frightful to behold them, and they'll be but very little stronger, I reckon, when plastered over and made to look substantial." Despite such criticism, public and private, the Grace Church contract was of inestimable value to a young man just beginning his career as an architect. Grace was, in the words of Philip Hone, "to be a fashionable church, and already its aisles are filled . . . with gay parties of ladies in feathers and mouse-line-de-laine dresses, and dandies with mustaches and high-heeled boots."[22]

While Grace was still under construction, Renwick began two other New York churches. For the Church of the Puritans, in that "new and remote part of the city called Union Square," Renwick abandoned the Gothic style used on Grace, selecting instead the style variously referred to as Norman, Lombard, or Romanesque (fig. 10). Instead of the pointed arches for windows and doors as for the Gothic Grace Church, Renwick here used rounded-head windows and doors throughout. The architect rather arbitrarily applied crenelation across the main façade at the level where the two towers rose from the body of the church. Between the two towers was an extremely crowded gable, with corbel coursing just over three rounded-head windows that rested on the crenelation. No spires were built for the towers. The left tower rose one stage above the body of the church, as opposed to two stages for the right tower, although a sloping roof on the left tower somewhat balanced the composition. Marble was used only on the front and right façades of the exterior, to save money; brick and plaster covered the rear and the left façades that adjoined an existing building. As on Grace, the interior columns were of plaster, and Renwick produced the whole for $40,000. His sources for the church in general and the gable arrangement in particular were the Romanesque churches of Germany, which had been illustrated in the second volume of Thomas

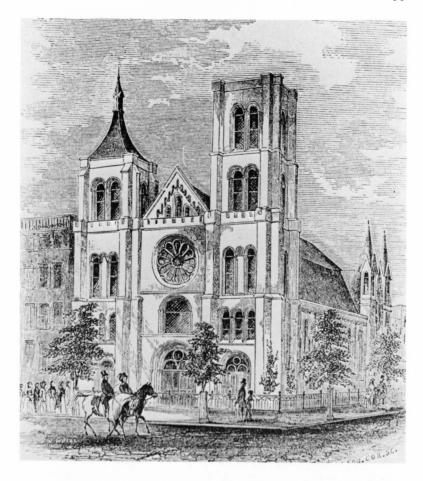

Figure 10. James Renwick, Jr., Church of the Puritans, New York. 1846.

Hope's *Historical Essay on Architecture* (fig. 11). By reproducing numerous Romanesque designs Hope inspired the succeeding generation of architects to revive the rounded arch in a style referred to as *Rundbogenstil.* Hope was also to be a profound influence on the architectural thought of Robert Dale Owen.[23]

Renwick also benefited from family connections in procuring the commission for Calvary Church. The founder of the church, the Reverend John McVicar, was professor of moral philosophy at Co-

Figure 11. Dom of Mayence.

lumbia, and thus colleague to Renwick senior and teacher to Renwick junior. Although he returned to the Gothic fold for Calvary, Renwick chose to experiment with the early English variety of Gothic, with considerably less ornamentation. Moreover, while the influence of Pugin is still evident, the twin spires suggest the inspiration of continental Gothic as well. The cornerstone was laid in March 1846 by the Episcopal bishop of New York, and the edifice rose in little more than a year. After its consecration, the *New York Post* mentioned that the "new and splendid church of the Calvary . . . has drawn off some of the fashion from Grace Church." Young Renwick probably did not mind that Calvary might draw well-to-do parishioners away from Grace: Calvary still owed him for "carpets, furniture, insurance, architect's fee and organ." So great were the debts that the church was forced to rent pews, much as Grace Church did. In addition, the rectory was far from completion and even farther from payment. The vestry of the church solved the problem by conveying the rectory "to the builder on the condition that he should complete it, and he then leased it to the church until such time as they could pay for it."[24]

Renwick was collecting prestige and IOU's from the various churches of New York at a brisk pace, but his old classmate George Templeton Strong was not impressed. He called Calvary Church a "miracle of ugliness" and wrote that the Church of the Puritans gave "hopeful indications of being somewhat worse."[25] Strong loved to ridicule Renwick and his work, but even as Calvary was rising, Renwick was devoting his attention to his plans for the proposed Smithsonian Building. He concluded that he would offer not one but two ways of covering the floor plan of David Dale Owen, one in the Gothic and another in the Norman style. His competition entries were in Washington by late November 1846.

The regents gathered once again on November 30, 1846, this time in the rooms of the board's vice-president in the Capitol Building. All but four were present: William Campbell Preston continued to be ill, and Chief Justice Roger B. Taney was riding circuit; Senator George Evans and Rufus Choate would arrive on December 1 and 2, respectively.[26]

Chancellor George M. Dallas read the report of the building committee to the assembled regents. The report summarized the travels of the subcommittee in September, and noted that the "architects with whom [Mr. Owen] conferred are required to transmit their several plans to the Board by the 25th of December next. Until they are received, no definite choice can be made." Despite this clear-cut statement, the report of the committee was followed by an oral report: "The Committee unanimously selected, out of thirteen plans that were submitted to them by some of the principal architects throughout the country, two by Mr. James Renwick, Jr., of the city of New York, the architect of Grace Church, the Church of the Puritans, Calvary Church, and other structures, in and near New York; and they recommend to the Board for adoption one of these, being a design in the later Norman, or, as it may, with more strict propriety, be called, the Lombard style, as it prevailed in Germany, Normandy, and in Southern Europe in the twelfth century." Although no *definite* choice could be made by the regents, the building committee seized the opportunity to *recommend* one of the plans in a display of unanimity calculated to influence the rest of the regents. The impression that the committee was attempting to give Renwick's design the upper hand while not officially declaring it as chosen was further heightened by the statement that "contracts are not yet made," implying simultaneously that they were soon to be made and that the building committee had the authority to make them, which they did, but only after the approval of the plan by the entire board.

Owen had pressed his case in a most daring manner. In less than three months he had in hand a set of plans in the style that he had originally favored, and he had stolen the rhetorical march on all of Renwick's competitors. This succeeded in making Renwick the leading candidate for the job, but it also succeeded in stirring up a tempest among those not used to the game of verbal brinksmanship at which Owen was so adept.

Chapter Three

🌿

A TEMPEST AMONG THE ARCHITECTS

No official mention of the election of a Secretary—the chief executive officer of the Institution—was made before December 1846, but electioneering had begun soon after the passage of the Smithsonian legislation. A. D. Bache used his influence with the other regents and a compromise with Choate and the library faction to insure the selection of Professor Joseph Henry of the College of New Jersey. Henry, deeply sceptical of the wisdom of commencing a large building, immediately came into conflict with Robert Dale Owen and James Renwick, Jr. The other competing architects were aware of Renwick's favored status and thus of their own lessened status, and sought to dislodge Renwick by undercutting his price. They succeeded in coaxing the regents to hear them out, but when the board finally gave their approval to Renwick's plan, some of the disappointed competitors vented their frustration in public. The regents, however, were unmoved, and preparations began for construction of the building.

Soon after President James K. Polk signed the Smithsonian Institution into existence, Francis Markoe, one of the founders of the National Institute and a clerk at the Department of State, wrote to his friend Richard Rush, discussing his chances of being named as the Secretary of the Smithsonian. Vice-President George M. Dallas had visited the president on the previous Sunday, and Polk had informed him that Markoe was the man for the position. "Mr. Dallas,

Col. Totten, Mr. Force and other friends are sanguine that I will succeed," Markoe wrote, "notwithstanding the list of competitors who are daily multiplying, and embrace men of rank High Standing, e.g. Prof. Henry of Princeton!" He feared that the "absence of some of my friends, such as Mr. Preston, Senator Breese, Mr. Hilliard . . . and others" might well jeopardize his chances of election. But Markoe was well aware that the greatest threat to his chances was not the absence of his friends but the presence of A. D. Bache. Markoe regretted that Bache had been appointed a regent, and found it "quite absurd" that he would be counted as a member of the National Institute. Bache had been a corresponding member but never a fierce supporter of the Institute. Markoe, however, had another reason for regretting Bache's presence on the board: "I fear him also, personally, because I have reason to believe that he will use all his exertion to secure the [appointment] of Prof. Henry."[1]

Bache had indeed requested that his old friend Joseph Henry write down any thoughts he might have about the course which the Institution might take. Henry had been professor of natural philosophy at the College of New Jersey in Princeton for the past fourteen years. Before that, he had taught at the Albany Academy, in Albany, New York, where he himself had been educated. Henry's principal area of research was physical science, particularly in electromagnetism. His discoveries in the field led to their practical application by Samuel F. B. Morse in the telegraph.[2]

Henry believed that the mission of Smithsonian was more closely related to the increase rather than the diffusion of knowledge. "There are at this time," he wrote to Bache, "thousands of institutions actively engaged in the diffusion of knowledge in our country, but not a single one which gives direct support to its increase." This severe imbalance, Henry thought, was a result of the excessively pragmatic American character, in that "original discoveries are far less esteemed among us than their applications to practical purposes, although it must be apparent on the slightest reflection that the discovery of a sure truth is much more difficult and important than any one of its applications taken singly." Some of the inducements used in Europe to promote scientific investigation were, Henry said, "incompatible with the genius of our institutions."[3]

The various facets of the Smithsonian program—a library, a museum, a series of popular lectures—struck Henry as being essentially local, that is, diffusing knowledge only to those who lived close enough to Washington to take advantage of a library or lectures. This same concern most likely motivated Robert Dale Owen's proposal for a normal school, which would spread teachers across the land and thus more effectively diffuse knowledge. Henry's chief concern, on the other hand, was to facilitate basic research by creating a national intellectual forum in the form of a new journal. This journal would treat not only the physical sciences but also moral and political science and the fine arts. A library, a museum, and other research facilities were useful adjuncts to original scientific investigation, Henry insisted, but they must remain subordinate to the active efforts to increase knowledge. The result of such "active operations" could then be diffused through the journal, which would be offered "at prices so low that they would be within the reach of almost every person. . . ."

Henry's emphasis on the Smithsonian as a clearinghouse of knowledge rather than a library and museum open to all necessarily lessened the need for a separate Smithsonian Building. The Princeton professor hoped "that but a very small part of the present interest will be expended in putting up a building; it is to be regretted that the institution cannot be accommodated with some rooms of the present public buildings. . . . The name of Smithson is not to be transmitted to posterity by a monument of brick and mortar, but by the effects of his institution on his fellow men." Henry was very familiar with monuments of brick and mortar, for he had taught the class on architecture at Princeton in the 1830s.

For all his willingness to offer suggestions, Henry had no great desire to become the first Secretary. He vowed not to think of the matter unless he could "be assured that the situation will be independent of party politics." In particular, Henry did not wish to be "disturbed by every change in the politics of the majority of the board." Even on the day before the regents voted for Secretary, Henry expressed doubts that the financial arrangements would be satisfactory. To his brother James, Henry wrote that he would "not venture to remove to Washington for 3000 dollars. I am promised an increase of salary at Princeton and in consideration of the greater expense the addition would not be much." Henry believed deeply in the promotion of scientific research, but he had no desire to engage in political battles in the name of science.[4]

Francis Markoe was encouraged by word of Henry's hesitance. In mid-October he wrote to Rush, "*In confidence!*", that Henry did not seek the job and that he would never be prevailed upon to leave Princeton. Markoe had heard this through his friend "Capt. Chauncey of the Navy who had it from Lt. David Porter of the Navy, and he learned it at the Walkers and said that it was told that family by A. D. Bache himself." Bache, meanwhile, was busily agitating for Henry. The balance rested with Rufus Choate and the library faction.[5]

The meeting of December 3 started well for Bache. Robert Dale Owen offered a resolution from the Committee on Organization, declaring that the Secretary of the Smithsonian Institution should "possess eminent scientific and general acquirements; that he be a man capable of advancing science and promoting letters by original research and effort, well qualified to act as a channel of communication between the institution and scientific and literary individuals and societies in this and foreign countries." That is, the Secretary should be everything that Henry was and Markoe was not. Owen thus revealed himself as a Henry supporter, and the tally on the resolution immediately became a test vote. With the passage of the resolution, Owen quickly moved to postpone consideration of the other resolutions on organization and instead to elect a Secretary.[6]

As the regents marked their ballots, several things were working against Markoe. His friend William Campbell Preston was still in South Carolina, too ill to attend. His friend George M. Dallas, Chancellor of the Institution, was the chairman of the meeting, and could not vote unless in the case of a tie, and then Dallas would have met with intense lobbying from his nephew, Bache. But most importantly, Bache had come to an agreement with Choate over the library.

The final vote read: Henry 7, Markoe 4, and 1 for Charles Pickering, who had served briefly as the curator of the National Institute. Markoe's supporters were probably Breese, Hilliard, Rush, and Totten. Henry received the votes of Bache and Hawley—the only two regents he knew personally—Owen, Hough and Choate, and two of the remaining three: Evans, Pennybacker, and Seaton.[7]

Bache wrote to Henry the next day, relating the decision of the board and the bargain struck with Choate and the "book men." The regents offered Henry $3500 and a house to become the Secretary.

Bache explained that Henry was expected to nominate an assistant secretary, who would be in charge of the library. "Charles C. Jewett of Brown is the man whom the library part of the Board desire to have chosen & indeed a majority of the Regents. You will conciliate them by nominating him. He is in every way worthy of your choice." Nevertheless, Bache sought to emphasize the political import of the nomination, as he had taken "pains to ascertain the wishes of many of the *book men* with whom we have crossed swords, & whose good will to you it was important to secure."[8]

Even before Henry received the news, the issue of the library erupted when the regents took up consideration of resolution number one from the Committee on Organization. Owen suggested the appropriation of $20,000 over and above the salary of the librarian for the "gradual fitting up of a library." Hough, who had been Owen's ally throughout the year, moved that the amount be reduced to $12,000. This did not violate the letter of the agreement with the book men, but it must have roused them, for the amendment was voted down. Rush, who had voted for Markoe and was thus not subject to the agreement, suggested that $15,000 be substituted in the resolution. This too failed, and the book men got their full $20,000. Even this sum was less than the $25,000 stipulated in the congressional legislation, but the book men must have felt that they could make it up after the completion of the building, when they would have a library ready to fill. Two further resolutions must have soothed the book men, one calling for the Secretary to employ an assistant secretary for the library and another creating a committee to make a list of books to be purchased for the Institution.[9]

With some sort of equilibrium established between the book men and the other factions, the regents adjourned on December 5. They were, Bache wrote to Henry, "in the best possible humor with themselves for having done so fine a thing as to elect you their [Secretary], thus paying homage to Science as the Chancellor expressed it shaking his antonine curls while bowing reverently." The news of Henry's election had already appeared in Seaton's *National Intelligencer*, and Bache sent a copy to Princeton. He concluded his letter to the Secretary-elect by informing him that in Washington the "cry is now huzza for Henry. I say huzza for science which means the same."[10]

Henry accepted the appointment, hoping, as he wrote in strict confidence to Professor Asa Gray of Harvard, to save the "generous bequest of Smithson from utter waste." If left unmolested by politicians and their ilk, the Institution could be "of the highest importance to the science of our country and aid the labours of every true working man of science." But Henry foresaw difficulties if a large building consumed most of the funds. Indeed, he told Gray that if the "money is to be squandered on brick and mortar at Washington I shall resign."[11]

Henry's wariness of large buildings was confirmed in his eyes by the observations of his fellow scientist Charles Lyell. Henry owned a copy of Lyell's *Travels in North America*, of which an American edition had been published in 1845. Lyell discussed the Girard College affair as a cautionary tale for those who imagined that a "donation might be so splendid as to render an anti-building clause superfluous." Lyell argued that new institutions must strive for excellence in their programs while quartering in modest circumstances, then reaping the pecuniary benefits of their well-founded reputations. "None would then grudge the fluted column, the swelling dome, and the stately portico," Lyell concluded, "and literature and science would continue to be the patrons of architecture, without being its victims."[12]

Henry was painfully aware of the Girard fiasco before reading Lyell's account; his friend Bache had been president of the college during a portion of the building's construction. Bache had eventually resigned rather than wait for the completion of the building. The moral that Lyell drew from the Girard case was not lost upon Henry, nor was Lyell's eloquent language: in the heat of debate over the Smithsonian Building, Henry would write to his wife, Harriet, that "I can say with Mr. Lyell though I am an admirer of good building yet I do not choose to be its victim."[13]

Henry and Lyell insisted that a large and impressive building should be erected only after an institution had proven its merits. Henry's attitude towards the function of the Smithsonian was analogous to his view of architecture. Rather than diffuse preexisting research, he wanted the Institution to encourage original research, the data of which would be used to reach new conclusions and hence increase knowledge; the diffusion would come through the publications of the Institution, only after new discoveries had been made. With regard to the building, Henry did not want the Institution to adopt a preexistent form—the platonic ideals of the classical as proposed by A. J. Davis or the medieval as proposed by Robert Mills—which could not reflect in more than a general way the functions of the Institution, much less be a reflection of its success in carrying out those functions. Henry firmly believed that the actual institution must precede the building which symbolizes as well as houses it. In his attitude toward the Institution and toward its building, Henry was ever the empirically oriented scientist.

While Henry was in transit from Princeton, Bache received a letter from Thomas U. Walter, the very architect whom Nicholas Biddle had pushed into using an elaborate Corinthian design for Girard College. Bache and Walter had inspected a school and a hospital in London while they were both in the employ of the college. Walter now wished to know if the competition for the Smithsonian was still open, as the newspapers suggested. In September Walter had returned to Philadelphia to find a "polite note" from Bache, the cards of Owen and Hough, and word that "they would see me on their return." When no return visit materialized, Walter assumed that another architect had been engaged. He told Bache "somewhat confidentially" that he had a "great desire to obtain some engagement that would make it worth while for me to remove my family" from Philadelphia. With the completion of Girard College finally in sight, Walter had looked around to discover that there was "little or nothing doing in the way of architecture in Philadelphia and no prospect of improvement." Bache must have been quite honest in his reply, for Washington saw nothing of Walter for several years. [14]

Henry arrived in Washington on December 14, and the next day went with Bache and Owen to examine the ground on which the building was to be placed. A few days later he wrote to his wife, Harriet, that all the regents "with whom I have yet conversed have adopted my views," but cautiously added that those "of the Board who are absent will be of another opinion." Henry found the regents willing to "curtail their plans as much as possible so that the annual interest . . . will be used for carrying on the Institution." In relating some recently received advice that he should not be "too urgent" in pressing for the adoption of his plans, Henry sounded cool and Bache-like. "The Regents will soon weary of the affair and then I can direct the institution in the way I think best for the interest of science and the good of mankind." The great danger, Henry insisted in another letter, was that the regents might "think themselves obliged by the law to go on with the construction of a magnificent building."[15]

So energetic was Henry in pursuit of his objectives that he bypassed a great dance at the President's House to spend a peaceful evening lobbying at Colonel Totten's. Bache had been doubtful about Totten's attitude toward Henry and his plan, since the Colonel had voted for Markoe, but the Secretary found him "disposed to listen and in the end he gave his decided approval to the plan." Totten praised Henry's enthusiasm and told him that he was "just the man we want." Henry had won over an important ally in the chief of Army Engineers.[16]

Another interview was not so congenial, though Henry did not seem distressed by the result. Charles C. Jewett, the candidate of the book men for assistant secretary, visited Henry on the nineteenth. "I found him a very pleasant gentleman and had a long talk with him," Henry wrote to Harriet. "Gave him my views candidly and received from him an equally frank response. I think our views are so adverse that he will not accept the appointment." Nevertheless, Henry expressed some liking for Jewett and vowed to do what he could to secure him a commission which would allow him to begin work on the library.[17]

The new Secretary officially took up his duties at the meeting of December 21, 1846, a meeting devoid of substantive decisions. Henry Hilliard presented a letter from the Philadelphia architect Napoleon LeBrun "asking if the plan for the building was open to competition." Hilliard had replied that the Executive Committee was receiving plans until December twenty-fifth.[18]

The next meeting, on December 23, brought auspicious news. The regents' request for the rights to the land between Ninth and Twelfth Streets, some sixteen acres, had been accepted by President Polk and his cabinet. The opposition of Secretary of State James Buchanan and Commissioner of Patents Edmund Burke had thwarted two earlier proposals. The first claimed one hundred acres along the east-west axis of the public grounds stretching from Seventh Street to the river, excepting the ground set aside for the Washington Monument; the second requested land between Seventh and Twelfth Streets, about fifty-two acres. Ironically, the cabinet, after rebuffing a delegation of regents for the second time, decided in secret that they would accede to a request for the thirty-two acres between Twelfth and Fourteenth Streets, but the regents settled for sixteen acres. With the news that Polk had ratified their selection of a site, the regents adjourned until January twentieth.[19]

Later that evening of December 23, Isaiah Rogers arrived at Washington. He had given Owen some rough sketches of his proposal on September 22 but since then had worked long and laboriously on more detailed plans. These he presented to Owen on Christmas Eve, but Rogers left the meeting troubled, for "things looked as though they had their plan in view." Rogers saw the other plans for the first time on the day after Christmas. "Very handsomely drawn," Rogers thought. "Prospective plans colored up . . . very pretty to look at."[20]

Rogers discovered that John Notman, Owen G. Warren, and the firm of Wells and Arnot had submitted Gothic plans. John Haviland, like Rogers himself, submitted a plan in the Norman style. James Renwick had submitted plans in both styles. The only non-medieval entry was by Howard Daniels, one of the Cincinnati architects Owen had visited, who offered an "Italian" design, probably similar to Notman's Athenaeum in Philadelphia. All of the other architects had taken the advice of the Owen brothers and produced long, narrow, three-story buildings in a medieval style.[21]

The central section of John Notman's design recalled that of Town, Davis and Dakin for New York University: two towers flanked a large bay window that rose from the entrance to the roof line (fig. 12). Surmounting the central section was a Gothic tower reminiscent of Robert Mills's Smithsonian project, but taller, more sophisticated, and more archaeologically correct. Both of Notman's wings were ten bays wide—twice that of NYU—and at each end projections were created by moving three bays forward by one bay. Battlements adorned the roof, and finials resting on engaged buttresses rose above the crenelation.

Twin Gothic spires formed the ends of a tripartite central block in the scheme of Owen G. Warren, who had served as a draftsman for A. J. Davis in the early eighteen forties (fig. 13). A gable with a crocket and finial bridged the towers over a recessed entrance. The similarity of Warren's towers to those of the Gothic design of Renwick, and the use of a tripartite central block, so close to the entrance motif of Renwick's Norman plan, suggests that Warren fol-

Figure 12. John Notman, Proposed Smithsonian Building. North elevation. 1846.

Figure 13. Owen G. Warren, Proposed Smithsonian Building. North elevation. 1846.

49

lowed closely the guidelines offered by the Owen brothers. Eager to
please, his wings were even longer than Notman's, stretching for
some twelve bays. Other elements show that Warren was not used
to designing on so grand a scale. On the long north façade, several
doors opened at ground level, and on the west wing, a two-story
covered porch of a rather domestic appearance wrapped around a
projecting wing. The engaged buttresses rose above the battlement
and gave way to giant finials which broke the line of the plain pitched
roof. The confident hand of a Notman was simply not present.

Renwick, too, had opted for a long and narrow building, in both
his Gothic and Norman designs (figs. 14–17). On the former he
avoided the repetitiousness and horizontality of the elongated wings
by carefully defining them, through an emphatic two-bay deep projection and through subsidiary towers which rose well above the
roofline. Whereas Notman and Warren's battlements were cluttered
with crockets and finials, Renwick reserved these motifs for the wings
proper, for the main spires, and for the rest of the five-bay entrance.
His Norman design elaborated still further on the wings, making
them smaller but separated from the main building by one-story
connecting segments, called "ranges," similar to those David Dale
Owen had proposed. The towers were even more varied than on the
Gothic plan, although the two towers over the entrance were com-
pressed into a three-bay arrangement, as opposed to the five bays for
the Gothic. Both plans showed young Renwick developing a sense
for the dramatic arrangement of masses.

Isaiah Rogers proposed a building with a battlemented tower, a
mixture of pointed and rounded-head windows, and crenelation
throughout (fig. 18). His plan also included a porte cochere, as did
both of Renwick's offerings. Indeed, the competition entries re-
sembled each other much more closely than they did either New
York University or Robert Mills's earlier Smithsonian project. The
spirit of the Owen brothers, David Dale and Robert Dale, was clearly
at large among the competitors.

That evening, Rogers visited the home of William P. Elliot, the
draftsman who had won the competition for the Patent Office in
1836 only to see Robert Mills appointed supervising architect and
then radically alter the plans. Elliot now commiserated with Rogers
as they discussed how "to counteract the clique in the city in favor
of Mills and of Mr. Renwick."[22]

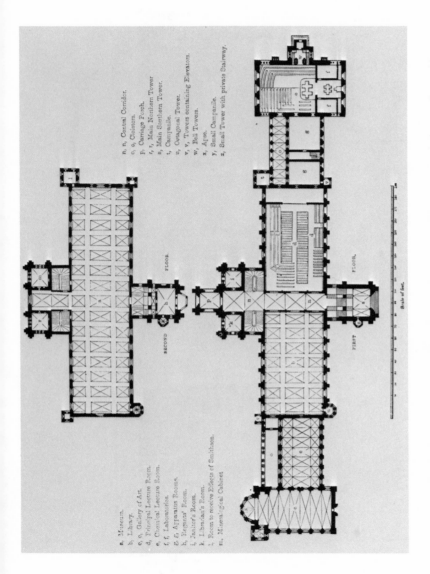

a, Museum.
b, Library.
c, c, Gallery of Art.
d, Principal Lecture Room.
e, Chemical Lecture Room.
f, f, Laboratories.
g, g, Apparatus Rooms.
h, Regents' Room.
i, Janitor's Room.
k, Librarian's Room.
l, Room to receive Effects of Smithson.
m, Mineralogical Cabinet.

n, n, Central Corridor.
o, o, Cloisters.
P, Carriage Porch.
r, r, Main Northern Tower.
s, Main Southern Tower.
t, Campanile.
u, Octagonal Tower.
v, v, Towers containing Elevators.
w, Bell Towers.
x, Apse.
y, Small Campanile.
z, Small Tower with private Stairway.

SECOND FLOOR.

FIRST FLOOR.

Scale of feet.

Figure 14. David Dale Owen–James Renwick, Jr., Smithsonian Building. Ground plan. 1845–1846.

51

Figure 15. James Renwick, Jr., Adopted Norman design, Smithsonian Building. North elevation. ca. 1847.

Figure 16. James Renwick, Jr., Adopted Norman design, Smithsonian Building. South elevation. ca. 1847.

Figure 17. James Renwick, Jr., Proposed Gothic design, Smithsonian Building. View from the northwest. ca. 1846.

Figure 18. Isaiah Rogers, Proposed Smithsonian Building. East elevation. 1846.

54

Soon after, young Renwick himself arrived in Washington, bearing a gift for Gideon Hawley and letters of recommendation which signaled a change in strategy. The letters were for Gideon Hawley and Daniel Webster, who was a close friend and former colleague of Rufus Choate. The author of the letters, the diplomat and Whig politician Luther Bradish, insisted to both men that despite the "sharp rivalry" which the junior Renwick faced in Washington, the architect did not "ask or desire for him or his plan anything more than a fair and open competition." The letters dwelled on the high character of Renwick and the regents to the point that the issue seemed to be moral rather than aesthetic. Except for two phrases in the four-hundred-word letter to Webster, Renwick might well have been applying for a ministerial position. With scandal already in the offing, Renwick could hardly ask for special consideration, and so his letters of recommendation beat a hasty retreat, attempting to set a tone of propriety and fair play.[23]

Renwick and his allies were not well coordinated, though. Isaiah Rogers called on Owen New Year's Day and was told that "they had selected Mr. Renwick's plans and that he was going to set about revising his plan and reducing the thing to the sum proposed." Apparently Renwick drew new Norman elevations without a third story in the main building. To confuse matters even more, Representative Cranston of Rhode Island reported back to Rogers the same day about a visit he had paid to Colonel Totten. Cranston said that "Totten had assured him that no plan had been adopted and that all confidence was placed in my ability and experience."[24] Totten, as an ally of the new Secretary, was determined to leave the impression that the regents had not settled upon Renwick's plan, or any other plan for a large building.

Other architects were arriving in town, and Rogers traded rumors with them. The New York architect David Henry Arnot and his partner Joseph Wells spent a long evening with Rogers, discussing word that the Executive Committee had chosen four designs which would be rewarded with premiums. Rogers's anxieties were fueled on January 5 when William Elliot claimed to have heard Regent William J. Hough say that Rogers "could not design a building," and that he "was only capable to erect buildings."[25] Continuing his alliance with Owen, Hough sought to downplay the talents of the other competitors to the advantage of Renwick.

Things began to look a little more hopeful for Rogers when Mayor Seaton gave him "some encouragement" that he would have some chance of success. But other than importuning the regents for some hint on their choice of an architect, there was little the assembled architects could do to expedite the decision. Arnot and Rogers dreamed about establishing an architectural society of the United States, which could presumably do something about expensive fiascoes like the one in which they were currently embroiled. The architect's irritation with the Executive Committee was increasing as Joseph Henry returned to the capital.[26]

Henry immediately immersed himself in electioneering on the building and working with Owen on the preparation of his report to the regents on "Organization." With the regents scheduled to meet in four days, Henry feared that it would "be impossible for me to prevent a large expenditure in the way of a building" without involving the Congress, a dangerous proposition considering the narrow margin of passage the enabling legislation had received.[27]

On the eighteenth, the Secretary received a visit from Owen, who showed Henry the plan of the building as cut down by young Renwick. "It is certainly beautiful," Henry conceded to his wife, "but will cost in its present state 202 thousand dollars." Henry did have some further alterations in mind, though. "I hope however to see the wings cut off and then it will probably cost 150 thousand."[28]

On the evening of the nineteenth, Henry dined at the home of Congressman Joseph Ingersoll of Pennsylvania with Mayor Seaton and Richard Rush. Perhaps the most pleasant thing about it, for the Secretary at least, was the discovery that "Mr. Rush has fully adopted my plan and will I have no doubt second all my movements." But Henry's letter was silent on whether Seaton adopted his plan. Instead he anticipated his next catechumen, General Lewis Cass, Senator from Michigan and freshly appointed regent, replacing the late Isaac Pennybacker. Henry met with Cass before the opening session began and was pleased to find that he opposed both a large library and an expensive building—most especially the building. Henry had another convert.[29]

Yet another Henry man was Judge Sidney Breese, the senator from Illinois. Breese, Henry was sure, "goes strongly against the building and will probably be pitted against Mr. Seaton." The Secretary began to grow hopeful that the "building, though large and extensive, will be less by nearly a half than at first contemplated."[30]

On January 20, 1847, the regents finally began the session. Attendance was good, but not complete, and, thought Henry, little progress was made. Choate, Hawley, Taney, and Preston were yet to arrive, and Colonel Totten had been called away to the Mexican War. Even were Totten present, Owen, Hough and Seaton could still call the architectural tune on the building committee, and so the chancellor read the report of the committee and introduced several resolutions. The committee urged that the Norman plan furnished by Renwick, amended as suggested by the committee—that is, without a third floor in the main building—be adopted, and that premiums of $250 be awarded to Wells and Arnot, John Notman, John Haviland, and Owen G. Warren. Unlike the committee's report of November 30, the decision was not unanimous. The regents ordered that consideration of the resolutions be postponed.[31]

Later in the meeting, Henry Hilliard presented to the regents a letter from John Haviland, offering to modify his plans as well, thus reducing the cost of his proposal. A price-cutting war seemed under way when Owen presented a printed letter from Wells and Arnot containing a precise breakdown of costs, which amounted to $192,000. Wells and Arnot noted that they had gone below the $250,000 figure provided by the regents because that body "would not deem it necessary to expend more for the necessary accommodations for the Institution than the *value* of these accommodations would warrant."[32]

Seaton, although in favor of Renwick's design, saw no other option than to recognize what Henry described as "quite a tempest among the architects," and moved that the board would hear any explanations that the architects might wish to provide. "The Board agreed to suffer each architect to be heard tomorrow in succession," Henry wrote that night, "and I presume we shall then have quite a series of lectures on the esthetic."[33]

The remaining architects converged on the Capitol the next morning at ten. David Arnot had remained in Washington while his partner Joseph Wells returned to New York. The regents heard from John Haviland and John Notman, and they adjourned before Arnot could complete his presentation. Isaiah Rogers, after waiting all day, spent the evening with Notman and Arnot at Notman's room. On Friday the twenty-second, Arnot finished his talk, and

Rogers finally had his say. He was succeeded by Renwick, and then by William Archer, a Georgetown builder-architect who had submitted a plan and estimate to the Board of Regents the previous September, on the very day on which Robert Dale Owen presented the plans of his brother and Robert Mills. After the session, Rogers, Arnot, and Haviland, perhaps in a funereal mood, visited the Congressional Cemetery. Having communed with Nature, or perhaps with the dead, they returned to the city. Later in the day, Rogers met his fellow Bostonian Rufus Choate, who had just arrived in town. After a conversation about the building, Choate "expressed himself favorable" to Rogers's appointment as architect.[34]

Choate appeared at the Capitol Saturday morning, January 23, in time to hear the last of the architectural lectures, this one by Robert Mills. "The fever was high today for a large building," Henry observed. The regents examined the plans and debated among themselves, and Chancellor Dallas, Cass, and Breese all served notice that they intended to offer amendments to the resolution of the building committee, but the decision was again postponed and the regents adjourned until Monday. Henry spent the afternoon renewing his efforts "to allay the fever," and conversations with Justice Taney and Judge Breese encouraged him. Bache, however, was *"quite down in the mouth* about the Smithsonian."[35]

Procedural matters filled Monday morning, and an afternoon debate did not provide a resolution. On Tuesday, Chancellor Dallas offered resolutions which declared it "inexpedient and hazardous to appropriate" more than $100,000 on a building, and which asked John Haviland if he would be willing to construct the building he had shown to the regents for that sum. The resolutions were promptly tabled.[36]

Instead, the regents moved to consider organizational resolutions sponsored by Choate, which enumerated the "two principal modes" of increasing and diffusing knowledge: a great library, and the publication of transactions, reports, and any scientific papers funded by Smithsonian appropriations. On the motion of Henry Hilliard, the assistant secretary was to take up his position, salaried at $2000, when the building was "ready for the reception of the library." The Secretary was authorized to name the assistant secretary, and Henry promptly nominated Charles C. Jewett. The board approved the nomination, and they again took up the question of the building.[37]

Henry was amazed by the tenacity of the Renwick supporters. "The very salvation of the integrity of the union of the states is thought to be connected with a large building at Washington," he exclaimed in a letter home. Bache had come up with a plan to finance the building from the interest of the fund over a five-year period, thus preserving the capital, but Henry feared that "it will not carry and nothing but a large building immediately erected will satisfy the Washingtonians." The other regents were not becoming disinterested as Henry had hoped they would, and he began to console himself with the notion that his allies were "all the best men." As for the other side, Owen was possessed with an "architectural mania and were it not for this the builders would be in the minority."[38]

Ever mindful of the Girard College fiasco, Henry saw the building as a potential obstruction to his plans, if it absorbed all the funds, and premature in terms of the needs of the Institution. Owen, ever the optimist and still an admirer of Secretary Henry, nevertheless did not budge in his determination that a large and symbolically appropriate building should be immediately started upon. As the board faced the final decision on the building, friction was increasing between Owen and Henry.

Bache's plan for preserving the principal of the fund had drawn little attention from the other regents, but when Bache introduced a resolution on January 27 limiting expenditure on the building to $100,000, funding through the available interest suddenly seemed a viable option. "The whole matter settled down into a very harmonious and satisfactory arrangement," Henry noted, "and the probability is now that we shall all separate well pleased with the transactions." Construction was to be spread out over five years, with the wings to be built before the main building. Owen would have his large building, and Henry would have the capital of the Smithsonian fund, and, after five years, the interest as well. Another resolution created a new building committee of three which was empowered to select a supervisor of construction and enter into contracts; the committee was also to revise the specifications of the plans in consultation with the Secretary.[39]

Oddly, the resolutions did not name Renwick as architect of the project, although his plan was chosen. Isaiah Rogers wrote in his diary that evening that he "learned from Mr. Owen that they had

adopted Mr. Renwick's plan, but had decided on no plan to build
by. *No architect appointed.*" Apparently Owen claimed that Renwick
had won the competition, but that the plans were open to revision
before building commenced. Renwick had not been appointed architect, but he was actively involved with Henry and the building
committee in adjusting his design to suit two stories in the main
building instead of three. Renwick's official appointment came a
month later, when the building committee granted him $1800 a
year for "superintendence"—meaning a monthly visit to Washington—retroactive to the "day when his plan was adopted by the committee of five," that is, November thirtieth.[40]

The regents may have felt that they had come to a harmonious
conclusion, but it jangled the nerves of the other competitors. When
Isaiah Rogers saw David Arnot and John Haviland the next day, he
discovered that they had received $250, but that there were "no
prospects for me in any shape." Rogers persevered, however, pre-
senting a bill for his plans to Owen, which was referred to the
Regents, who referred it to the Executive Committee. Haviland
sent a memorial as well, protesting the size of the remuneration and
the general manner in which the competition had been run. John
Notman, who like Haviland and Arnot had been voted $250, pre-
sented his own bill to the regents.[41]

The tempest among the architects moved north when David Arnot returned to New York. He made no attempt to disguise his
irritation and set to work on a pamphlet attacking the regents.
George Templeton Strong, Renwick's old Columbia classmate, had
his ear out for any word from Washington, and he must have heard
of Arnot's complaints soon after the architect's return. On January
31, Strong wrote in his diary that "happily there's reason to believe
that the monkey who built" Calvary Church and the Church of the
Puritans "will not be allowed to build the Smithsonian Institution
after all."[42]

In February 1847, David Arnot brought out his pamphlet entitled *Animadversions on the Proceedings of the Regents of the Smithsonian
Institution in Their Choice of an Architect for Their Edifice at Washington.*
The tract mixed ire over the handling of the competition with dis-
gust over the style of architecture selected. Most troublesome to
Arnot was that the Executive Committee had allowed Renwick to
prepare "new designs"—that is, his cut-down version of the build-

ing—after the deadline for entries. The confusion that marred the month of discussion further intensified Arnot's desire for a consistent and fair manner of selecting plans and architects. Without a competition "regulated by printed instructions, and published to all," he wrote, the Board of Regents was "accountable to no one. Or in other words, like the Pope, immaculate." Arnot's sense of fair play exceeded his theological vocabulary, but his aesthetic sense was also offended by the end product of the chaotic competition, which he thought to be symbolic of the "barbarism" of the middle ages.[43]

The responses of the regents to these protests were low key. On February 20, they voted $250 to Isaiah Rogers and refused to offer one penny more to John Notman than the $250 which he had not yet collected. As to Arnot's charges, any attempt to refute them would merely prolong the dispute. Instead, Bache proposed that the building committee should produce a "brief treatise, to be entitled 'Hints on Public Architecture,'" which would be illustrated with the winning design and any other plans that were the property of the Smithsonian.[44] The book could take care of any charges of architectural barbarism, and emphasize the positive results of what had been a most clouded competition.

Chapter Four

✠

THE UNEASY ALLIANCE

THE regents had finally settled upon Renwick's plan, but much remained to be done before the building would be realized. There were contracts to let, and stone to be selected. Joseph Henry, moreover, still harbored hopes that he could curtail the building. Robert Dale Owen, enthusiasm unabated, was equally determined to see the building rise intact. Relations between Henry and Owen were delicate, and complicated further by the presence of the library faction. An uneasy alliance prevailed at least temporarily, but alluring professorships, electoral upsets, and strenuous political maneuvering were eventually to alter the balance of power on the Board of Regents, and drastically affect the course of the Smithsonian Institution and the interior of its building.

James Renwick, Jr., had drawn heavily on the earlier design of David Dale Owen for his own plan. Those features for which he was responsible obliterated the last vestiges of the initial Robert Mills plan. Renwick's main building* was 200 feet by 50, with the principal lecture room and the library on the first floor, and the museum running the length of the second. As in Owen's plan, the east wing contained the chemical lecture room and laboratories, and the east range was devoted to space for chemical apparatus. The gallery of

---

*Both Robert Dale Owen and Joseph Henry referred to the central section of the Castle as the "main building" as distinct from the wings and ranges. Out of respect for this rare case in which Henry and Owen were in agreement, the term is used throughout this volume.

art occupied both the west wing and range. To the north of each range were the cloisters that Owen had proposed, although Renwick abandoned the conservatories on the south side of the ranges. He did retain Owen's idea of a large square tower in the center of the south façade (fig. 19). In this tower was the Regent's Room, complete with Owen's oriel window. Both north and south towers housed staircases, but none was spiral as Owen had suggested.

The two central towers on the north façade varied dramatically from Owen's plan. Instead of a Millsian octagonal tower, with Owen's porte cochere on the ground level, Renwick devised a tripartite portal projecting out from the plane of the main building. Reminiscent of his Norman design for the Church of the Puritans in New York, two towers soared above a central gable (cf. figs. 20, 10). The northeast tower featured a slanting roof much like that on the Church of the Puritans, but an octagonal tower rose out of the square base of the northwest tower. Both towers were taller and more slimly proportioned than on the New York church, and the gable in between was more sharply pointed as well. As on the Church of the Puritans, three rounded-head windows nestled inside the gable, but the battlements that ran across the façade of the church were here reserved for the rest of the main building and the east wing. The porte cochere projected out from the central north bay, with crenelation, corbel coursing, and large rounded-head arches.

Renwick retained Owen's idea of a smaller tower at each corner of the main building, creating a dramatically different tower for each corner. The largest, on the northeast corner, was the campanile, which rose almost as high as the left main tower, and echoed its sloping roofline. A small octagonal tower was at the southwest corner of the main building, and the two smallest towers, containing manual elevators, graced the northwest and southeast corners.

The east wing, like the main building, featured crenelation and corbel coursing, and, reflecting the chemical laboratories inside, chimneys and a bell tower (see fig. 24) containing flues rose above the battlements. The high-ceilinged chemical lecture room occupied most of the east wing, though the southern third of the wing was divided into two floors for the laboratories and storage space. The west wing, one large room that would, with the west range, serve as the gallery of art, had no battlements, and instead featured a pitched roof and an apsidal projection at the north, giving a chapel-like effect. Another campanile, similar to yet smaller than the one at the northeast corner of the main building, adjoined the northwest corner of the west wing.

Thus, Renwick kept closely to the ground plan of David Dale Owen, with the major revisions being the absence of conservatories on the south façade and of a third floor for the main building, and the replacement of the single octagonal tower on the north façade by two towers in a tripartite arrangement. Renwick rejected Owen's occasional use of the pointed arch, instead mixing the earlier Norman with his own exuberant inventions for the eight various towers. Renwick was not solely responsible for the Smithsonian Building, but his flair for the dramatic manipulation of form gave the building its characteristic variety of outline.

Joseph Henry, however, had but one view of the building: that of a drain upon the bequest of James Smithson. In mid-March he wrote

Figure 19. Smithsonian Building. View from the southwest.

Figure 20. Smithsonian Building. Main entrance, north front.

that Robert Dale Owen was now "quite willing to give up his fantasy of the building provided there is any danger of anything like a blow-up." Indeed, Henry found the entire building committee to be "most modified in their view of the building. They do not intend to close the contract as soon as they intended and have promised to make no move without consulting me." So optimistic was Henry that he predicted that the committee would "consent to the calling of a new meeting of the board to reconsider the whole matter."[1]

Perhaps in discussing the building with Owen and the other regents, Henry had elicited their agreement as to the costliness of the design, and assumed that their recognition of the expense meant that they were unwilling to pay that price. For whatever reason, Henry miscalculated badly, for as he wrote bids were being received, and on March 18 William J. Hough and Renwick were authorized to draw up a contract. The lowest bid had come from the Washington firm of James Dixon & Company, $205,250. The committee discovered, "on inquiry," that James Dixon & Co. actually consisted of James Dixon of Washington and Gilbert Cameron of New York. The hidden partner had also submitted a bid under his own name, and had been involved in a bid for stonecutting, carpentry, and masonry, under the name of Butler, Adams & Cameron. Cameron was involved in no less than four of the sixteen bids.[2]

Both Gilbert Cameron and his partner on one of the bids, Horace Butler, were subcontractors on Renwick's Calvary Church. Yet another veteran of Calvary Church, the carpenter John Sniffen, had submitted two bids for the Smithsonian job, one for the carpentry and another for the tesselated floor. Butler did not win the bid that he made with Cameron, but Dixon and Cameron offered his name "as security for the faithful performance of the contract." So when Renwick presented the contract to Dixon and Cameron, he was dealing with at least one man whom he knew well.[3]

Joseph Henry was either not familiar with or not trusting of the pair, and when Dixon and Cameron met with the building committee on March 19, the Secretary relayed a message from Bache requesting that he be allowed to read the contract before the parties signed it. Henry explained that Bache, though in town, was ill, and could not attend the meeting. The contractors agreed to sign the document then, and to allow the signatures of the members of the building committee to be affixed the next day. After Bache's perusal of the contract, he suggested an additional clause dealing with the procedure for any "important alterations in the plans of the building, or in the time of its execution." In such a case, the contractors would "receive, *pro rata*, according to the prices agreed in the foregoing contract, for work executed, and reasonable damages, if the nature of the case justly demands it." Dixon returned the next day, March 20, to sign the "addendum," which the three members of the building committee then signed. Henry had managed to insert a legal proviso which would allow him to alter the building with no interference from the contractors.[4] This power he would exercise time and again on the Smithsonian Building.

While Henry and Bache examined the contract with a fine-toothed comb, the Owen brothers and James Renwick had been combing the countryside in search of the best materials for the building's exterior. Their attention eventually focused on Seneca Creek, adjacent to the Potomac in Montgomery County, Maryland. Young Renwick found himself quite taken with a buff-colored stone, which he felt surpassed "any stone I have yet seen in this country; resembling in hue that . . . so highly esteemed by the architects of the middle ages." Unfortunately, the stone was not present in sufficient quantities for the Smithsonian Building. In much greater supply were two varieties of dark sandstone also located in the same area. Specimen Number 18 was a deep red color, and the other, Specimen Number 19, was a darker, crimson shade which the Owen brothers dubbed lilac gray. After David Dale Owen conducted experiments to test the durability of the various stones, he recommended the lilac gray, which was "in the opinion of men of good judgment and taste, appropriate for the Norman style of architecture." On March 30, the building committee officially selected the lilac gray sandstone from the Seneca Quarry.[5]

Less than two weeks later, on April 8, James Dixon wrote the committee claiming that the strata of lilac gray sandstone at Seneca Creek "seems to be nearly exhausted." Soon after, the committee received another letter, this one from the owner of the quarry, John Peter, expressing alarm that Dixon had made but a "superficial examination of the quarries." Peter insisted that his quarry could provide the stone "in any quantity you may require," and dramatically confronted Dixon at a meeting of the building committee on April sixteenth. The committee reiterated its desire not to use a stone darker than Specimen Number 19, and promised Peter that a member of the committee and the architect would inspect the quarry personally before any decision was reached. That inspection did not occur until October, when Robert Dale Owen, Renwick, and Gilbert Cameron discovered that, contrary to the representations of Dixon, the quarries at Seneca seemed "to be absolutely inexhaustible."[6]

*Figure 21. George Perkins Marsh, United States Representative
from Vermont, Smithsonian Regent and book man.*

As preparations for construction of the Smithsonian Building moved
forward, Secretary Henry could console himself that things in general were looking up. He had just moved into Gadsby's Tavern, on
Pennsylvania Avenue at Sixth Street, N.W., which was the lodging
place of Chancellor Dallas, and Henry found it the "most pleasant
house" he had yet been in. "The affairs at Washington," he wrote to
Harriet, "appear in a more pleasant condition than at any previous
period." Henry's optimism was heightened by the return from Mex-
ico of Joseph Totten, newly promoted to the rank of brigadier general. Since Totten was on the Executive Committee and the building

Figure 22. Robert Dale Owen.

committee, Henry expected that "under his direction, all things will go properly." Finally Henry had someone he trusted on the building committee and at the construction site.[7]

On May 1, a public holiday was declared in honor of the laying of the cornerstone. The procession began at City Hall. The ranks of militia from the District of Columbia, lodges of Masons from Washington, Baltimore, and Alexandria, and three military bands stretched over a mile of the parade route. At the White House they were joined by the President, his cabinet, and the diplomatic corps, and the procession continued down Fourteenth Street to the building site. A stage had been erected and decorated with evergreens, and the "principal persons connected with the Institution" assembled on the platform. The crowd that witnessed the event was quite large: Joseph Henry guessed perhaps twenty thousand, which would have been almost half the city's residents. But even the more conservative figure of six thousand given in the *National Intelligencer* was declared to be "the largest ever." After "a very impressive and eloquent prayer" from a Methodist minister, the Reverend Mr. F. S. Evans, the Masons proceeded with the ceremonial laying of the stone. Then Vice-President Dallas rose to address the throng on the history, origin, and goals of the Institution.[8]

Dallas's oration touched upon the rationale for the style of architecture selected for the building, as he listed the aims which had always been "controlling and uppermost with the Regents": "to conform strictly to instructions, and yet keep within the pecuniary limit assigned to them; to provide the space called for, and yet to avoid even the appearance of unnecessary expansion; to combine solidity with architectural beauty and wholesome ventilation, and to satisfy at once true taste and stern economy by banishing useless embellishment. . . ."[9]

The regents' search had led to the Norman style, which recommends itself, Dallas said, "for structures like this, to the most enlightened judgment." Dallas proclaimed that the Norman style "harmonizes alike with the extent, the grave uses, and the massive strength of the edifice; it exacts a certain variety in the forms of its parts; and it authorizes any additions that convenience may require, no matter how seemingly irregular they may be." Although the figures of speech were those of the vice-president, the architectural ideas, particularly the latter point on the ease of additions, suggests that Dallas had listened well to the arguments of Robert Dale Owen.

Behind Dallas on the platform sat Joseph Henry, staring at the orator's white curls and wishing that he had been able to give the vice-president a "few hints which might have modified some parts" of the address. Given the Secretary's continuing opposition to the building itself, he may have found the vice-president's aesthetic analysis to be lacking. Henry consoled himself with the thought that speeches and celebrations of that kind are the "flourish of the moment and produce no lasting effect." So with much pomp and a little scepticism the construction of the building was under way.[10]

Exactly one month after the laying of the cornerstone, however, one of the two contractors dropped out of the project. James Dixon, who had been the front for one of Gilbert Cameron's bids, "informed the Board that the work would thereafter be conducted by Mr. Cameron alone." The members of the building committee seemed to take a defensive attitude toward Cameron's work. The committee's report for 1847 expressed satisfaction with the contractor, despite "occasional departures from the letter of the contract," which were "promptly remedied" whenever a complaint was made. Such faint praise, while hardly damning, did not bode well for the reliability of the contractor on future occasions. Henry remained somewhat optimistic about it all because of his deepening friendship with General Totten. "Bache told me that when we became acquainted with each other we would draw together," Henry confided to his wife. "Now that he is on the ground many things will go on well with reference to the building."[11]

Henry's letters to his wife in the spring of 1847 frequently dwelled upon his "duty to continue" as Secretary of the Smithsonian. But in June he faced a severe temptation in the form of the chair of natural philosophy at the University of Pennsylvania from which Dr. Robert Hare had recently resigned. "When I first heard of the resignation of Dr. Hare," he wrote to Bache, "a regret passed my mind that it had not taken place before my connection with Smithsonian." Although he was able to put such thoughts out of his mind, Henry began to receive letters from friends urging him to lay claim to the position. So concerned was Henry over his predicament that he made a special trip to Washington in order to confer with Totten, Seaton, and a few others. But a fatigue-inspired illness forced him to return to Princeton, and Henry once again turned to Bache for advice.[12]

Bache, from his summer home at the Coast Survey Station at Andover, fired off his response, imploring that Henry would "not think of looking back, now that you have your hand to the plough." He argued that the two situations were hardly comparable in terms of their potential benefit to science. "Turn not from the rising to the setting sun. Go not into an old institution to be shorn of emolument & uncertain for its connexion with those you cannot control, when you can *be* a new institution—ready to grow to your station."[13] Bache succeeded in convincing Henry of his indispensibility to the Smithsonian, and the Secretary turned down the offer at Pennsylvania.

Robert Dale Owen, campaigning for reelection in southwestern Indiana, returned to New Harmony in early August to find a letter from Seaton detailing Henry's indecision as to the position at Pennsylvania. Owen wrote to Bache two days later, confessing that portions of the letter gave him "considerable uneasiness." Owen was not surprised at any inclination on Henry's part to resign, and would "never blame him if he" did. The university chair was a more desirable one "for a man of Henry's temperament," would pay more, and offered the much more pleasant circumstances of Philadelphia. Opined Owen: "If he still remain with us, the Institution ought to consider itself, while he lives, as deeply his debtor." But the possibility of Henry's resignation seemed real to Owen, and he anticipated difficulties in finding a replacement. Neither Charles Jewett nor Francis Markoe seemed likely successors, especially given Jewett's one-sided connection with Choate and the book men. Owen placed his hopes on the possibility that Bache could find another man of science, "who, if not [Henry's] equal—that we cannot expect—shall yet fill, with honor to himself & credit to the Institution, his place."[14]

Henry wrote to Owen in early August, saying that he had turned down the post at Pennsylvania. The Secretary observed that the "fate of the Institution at present depends very much on a harmonious co-operation between you and myself." He reiterated his fear that the building would absorb so much of the Institution's income "that the scientific operations will be materially interfered with." Henry entreated Owen to "induce Congress to pay for the main building" or to finance the museum, after which "all will be well and you will deserve a statue in one of the niches of the Smithsonian edifice."[15] The Secretary's concern over the building remained strong, but he still sought an accommodation with Owen.

As he wrote, Henry did not know that, just a few days before, Owen had lost his bid for reelection, and would not be eligible for reappointment as a regent in December. The news did not hit the Eastern papers until two weeks later, August 14, 1847. On that day a friend wrote to Henry that Owen had lost to the Whig candidate by some two hundred votes. The Whig strategy had included readings from *The Free Enquirer*, Owen's radical journal from his

New York days. Horace Greeley delightedly wrote Owen's political obituary in the pages of the *New York Tribune*: "In his whole career as a public man, Mr. Robert Dale Owen exhibited himself as a simple, thoroughgoing average party hack, and not at all the Philosopher, the Philanthropist, the Reformer that he once professed to be and by many has been considered."[16]

Within forty-eight hours of the news of Owen's defeat, Henry was drawing up a new set of instructions for young Renwick. The Secretary wrote that he did "not wish the building pushed so rapidly as to dispose of much of our capital now in the form of Treasury notes." He did allow that the wings, which were then under construction, should be finished as soon as possible.[17] Nevertheless, the Secretary had moved quickly to fill the political vacuum that the anticipated departure of Owen from the Board of Regents created.

By mid-October, Henry was seriously contemplating the utilization of the clause which Bache had placed in the contract for the amendment of the plans of the building. Henry's suggestion was somewhat radical: abolish the main building completely and connect the two wings with a giant screen. In a letter to William Campbell Preston, Henry seemed confident that the move was legal. The contract, he wrote, allowed the "Regents, if they see fit, to abolish the main building, or to defer the time of its completion, provided the contractor is paid reasonable damages, to be assessed by persons chosen by the Board." Although he was by no means certain that his plan would be accepted by the board, Henry had no doubt as to the practicality of the plan. "The two wings joined together by a screen would form a symmetrical arrangement, and would be sufficient to answer to our purposes for years to come."[18] Even if the main building could not be entirely abolished, it could be delayed for several years, thus leaving time for more interest to accumulate.

When Henry returned to Washington in early December, he "found Owen busily engaged in devising a plan to increase the income of the Institution." The plan limited the initial outlays of the Institution for scientific research and the library so as to build up the principal until the completion of the building freed the rest of the interest. Henry paid little attention to the scheme until he discovered that "Owen had brought over every member of the Board in Washington," including Bache, to the plan. When Henry "found that it had the approbation of Bache, I was induced to look upon it with more favor." [19] By finding an equitable way of financing the building without disturbing the principal of the fund, Owen had eased whatever discontent existed on the board over the cost of the building, and thus prevented Henry from doing away with the main building and connecting the wings with a screen.

During the fall of 1847 the building progressed, but the members of the building committee, Seaton, Totten, and Owen, received allegations "by sundry individuals" that the contractor, Gilbert Cameron, was using materials of insufficient quality. An examination uncovered "some pieces of timber in the east range which were not merchantable." This was not serious enough to warrant the replacement of the lumber, but Renwick was admonished that in the future he should "throw out every piece of timber, no matter how unimportant its destination, which was not strictly merchantable." [20] This first hint of improprieties on the building site was to be by no means the last.

The annual meeting of the Board of Regents convened on December 8, 1847, with the membership of the board in a state of flux. Senator James A. Pearce of Maryland replaced George Evans, the senator from Maine, but the House had not yet named the replacement for the defeated Owen, or for Hough, who had not run for reelection. So for the first few days of the session, reports were heard and debated from the building committee and the Secretary. On December 13, Owen asked to be excused from the Executive Committee, a motion which was, to the consternation of Henry, denied by the regents. They did, however, allow General Totten to remove himself from the committee since, he claimed, the building committee took up all his available time. Bache was elected in Totten's place on the Executive Committee, and at the next meeting Bache introduced the resolutions on appropriations for the coming year. [21]

Things began to fall apart for Henry at the next meeting. Hough introduced two resolutions which declared that Richard Rush, who had been appointed minister plenipotentary to France, was no longer a regent, and that Robert Dale Owen should be proffered to the Senate as a replacement. Both resolutions passed. Perhaps attempting to put the best face on the situation, Bache moved that Rush be named an honorary regent. That was approved, as was a Seaton motion that the chancellor should write to Rush explaining the whole affair. As if to forestall any more bad news, Henry then produced a telegram from Rufus Choate in Boston, pointedly addressed not to the Secretary but to "Professor Jewett," announcing simply "I will be in Washington on Monday." The regents promptly adjourned until Tuesday.[22]

Henry was taken aback. "I had no idea at first that Mr. Owen could have any chance of getting onto the Board after his time expired," he wrote to Asa Gray. "Mr. Rush has signified a desire to remain a Regent during his absence and there was therefore apparently no vacancy." But the friends of Hough and Owen had prevailed on the resolution, which nevertheless still faced congressional approval. Henry for his part was determined to exact some price for the victory. "I had a free conversation with [Owen]," Henry recalled, "and insisted that he should resign his positions in the executive and organizing committees." Since this allowed Owen to concentrate his attentions on the building committee, the Indianan consented.[23]

On Tuesday Choate appeared and the regents discussed the resolutions on appropriations that Bache had introduced earlier. At a meeting held that evening, the resolutions passed. Bache then moved that the Secretary should inform Professor Jewett, who was eager to start work even before completion of the library in the west wing, that his duties and his salary would commence on March 19, 1849. This, too, the regents approved. Choate requested that the chancellor appoint a committee of three to determine what services might be rendered by Professor Jewett prior to his full employment. This resolution, at Choate's suggestion, was laid on the table for the time being.[24]

Owen, at the next meeting, kept his promise to Henry by renewing his effort to be excused from service on the Executive Committee. To the relief of the Secretary, he succeeded. This was to be Owen and Hough's last meeting, at least until Owen could be approved as Rush's replacement. Their respective successors would take their places the next day: Congressman Robert McClelland of Michigan, and none other than that notorious book man George Perkins Marsh of Vermont (fig. 21). No sooner did Henry find Hough and perhaps Owen out of his way than Choate and Marsh seemed on the verge of stepping over the boundaries of the uneasy alliance that had been maintained since Henry's election. Suspicion centered on Choate's resolution for determining what intermediate duties Jewett could pursue. Jewett was eager to be employed immediately, despite the terms of the agreement.

Among those concerned by the possibility of disintegration of the agreement was Robert Dale Owen. Early on Thursday morning, December 23, he wrote to Bache counseling that the resolution should be steered to the Executive Committee, where Bache and Seaton could bottle it up even if Pearce dissented. Owen further saw the possibility of the book men trying a "bolder game" and attempting "to reverse . . . important decisions," especially since Hawley and Pearce had already departed. "We waited for Choate," he reminded Bache, and the book men, he felt, should not take advantage of such a temporary imbalance. Bache was even given advice on a topic of which he was a proven master. "Don't let Henry get nervous, and talk of resigning, if things seem going wrong. It will be construed into a threat to do harm. I am satisfied, that by a little good management, all can be made to go right." Some twenty years before, a phrenologist had told Owen that his organs of benevolence, conscientiousness, and friendship were highly developed, and that of wit developed least of all, and Owen was proving it in 1847 by failing to realize that Henry was rapidly coming to despise both him and the building with which he was associated.[25]

The regents gathered at 10 A.M. Marsh and McClelland appeared, along with Henry Hilliard, who had been reelected and reappointed. They joined Dallas, Bache, Choate, Seaton, and Totten. Choate's resolution requesting clarification of Jewett's duties was taken up, and adopted. The chancellor appointed Choate, Bache, and McClelland to a committee which would determine what could be done with the library. Four days later the committee reported and the regents approved a list of catalogues and bibliographies that Jewett could purchase, and a committee was set up to oversee the work of the assistant secretary. Choate, Bache, and Marsh were appointed. Jewett could begin work, but not full time; this was a compromise that pleased everyone but Jewett himself. Having settled the question, at least temporarily, the regents adjourned until December 1848.[26]

Henry had been thwarted on the question of completing the building by Owen's financial maneuver, and almost worse, Owen might regain his place on the board. Henry was becoming increasingly resentful. In February 1848 he wrote to William Campbell Preston that the building was "going on as rapidly as could be expected and thus far it has not exceeded the amount of the contract." The estimate of the building committee had risen to $250,000, although Henry considered $300,000 more likely. Even if the building was completed using only the interest and preserving the principal, Henry now insisted that "every dollar thus improperly spent on local objects is a fraud on the cause of the increase and diffusion of knowledge among men." Nevertheless, he conceded that it was "impossible to stop the building, and all I can hope to do is restrain the tendency to further extravagance."[27]

But if Henry was resigned to tolerating the building, he was by no means prepared to accept Owen's reappointment. Preston had recently written Henry, submitting a letter of resignation along with it. For a number of reasons, Henry suppressed it. The letter came after the adjournment of the regents' annual meeting, "and as there will be no opportunity of placing it before the Regents until next December [of 1848] I have kept it myself," Henry wrote. Both Preston and Henry knew that the real reason lay elsewhere. "Were it known that you wished to resign there would be an effort made to put in a person more favorably disposed to pressing the completion of the building than to carrying out my plans." That is, Owen would be appointed in Preston's place. The South Carolinian had no objection to remaining on the board if Henry insisted, though his continued poor health would make his service to the Smithsonian little more than keeping Owen off the board.

Another vacancy had been created by the resignation of Senator Lewis Cass, a strong Henry man. His replacement turned out to be an even stronger Henry man: Jefferson Davis, one of the six congressmen from the deep south to vote for the establishment of the Smithsonian, and a close friend of Bache since their West Point days. Davis had once, despite a violent illness, made a speech on the Senate floor in favor of an appropriation for Bache's Coast Survey. He could be expected to be as devoted to Henry.[28]

The prime concern for Henry, though, was that Owen might be reappointed. Horace Greeley's *New York Tribune* had already warned, in late December, that Owen's reappointment might turn the Board of Regents into a "hospital for destitute politicians." Congressman Andrew Johnson of Tennessee, an original opponent of the Smithsonian bill, was making ominous sounds on the floor of the House concerning the Institution, and even though his resolution demanding an investigation of the affairs of the Smithsonian was tabled, some antipathy toward the Institution remained in the House, and Henry's concerns about Owen's controversial reputation were not simply delusive.[29]

The resolution which went to the Senate to fill the vacancies on the Smithsonian Board of Regents renominated Rufus Choate and Gideon Hawley, and suggested that Owen replace Rush. The Senate referred the bill to the Joint Committee on the Library, in which Senator Tappan had frustrated the National Institute some years before. Henry informed the chairman of the committee that the terms of Choate and Hawley were yet to expire, and the Secretary hoped that "their names will be struck off the resolution before it is reported to the Senate."[30]

The make-up of the Library Committee was extremely favorable to Henry's point of view on the nominations. The chairman was James A. Pearce of Maryland, a Smithsonian regent and an ally of Henry on the Executive Committee. Jefferson Davis was on the committee, as was William Ballard Preston, a Virginia cousin of William Campbell Preston. John G. Palfrey, a conscience—that is, antislavery—Whig from Massachusetts, had recently replaced John Quincy Adams on the committee, but did not improve Owen's chances. Palfrey, a minister, had been writing defenses of theological schools while Owen was writing anticlerical tracts. He was further indisposed to support Owen in light of the latter's vote against the Wilmot Proviso, the antislavery amendment attached to an appropriations bill for the Mexican War, which was a political litmus test for Palfrey. Owen, however, intensely desired to see the building through to completion, and his own allies had a number of alternative plots to hatch.

By the end of March 1848 Henry was courting Palfrey and other members of the committee. To Palfrey he wrote that "it is highly important that the nomination [Owen's] of which we spoke be stopped in the Library Committee." If the nomination were to be discussed on the floor of the House, Henry felt, it would "produce effects disastrous to the Institution in the angry excitement which would ensue." Henry begged Palfrey "not to mention my name in connection with this," at least not until the Secretary had had time to confer with Jefferson Davis.[31]

In addition to lobbying the members of the Library Committee, Henry decided to confront Owen himself. On the same day as his letter to Palfrey, Henry wrote to Bache, enclosing a letter he had written to Owen, which he submitted to Bache's "judgement as to the propriety of sending it. It is an honest expression of my opinion and though it may not give him pleasure it will do him no harm." The letter to Owen centered upon his earlier publications and his reputation at large and in the Congress. In particular Henry zeroed in on Owen's pamphlet *Moral Physiology*, a work almost eighteen years old, which had included a discussion of three modes of birth control, which, the Secretary claimed, "evidently teaches the means of enjoying the pleasures of illicit love without the fear of its penalties." As a result, Henry claimed, there was "much feeling in the House" relative to Owen's reappointment, and the Secretary feared that if the matter was reopened the consequences would "be disastrous to yourself and the Institution."[32]

The letter to Owen was sent, but did no good, for three weeks later Henry reported to William Campbell Preston that "great efforts" were being made by the friends of Owen and Hough to regain their positions, even though the Library Committee had "concluded that there was no vacancy." Hough, claimed Henry, had tried to make a seat for himself by writing to Gideon Hawley, who, as the private citizen from New York, held the only seat for which Hough was eligible, suggesting that he should resign. Also, Preston's friend Captain Wilkes was "exerting himself for the election of Mr. Owen." Wilkes, who was, as Henry reminded Preston, the uncle of young Renwick, and others were "afraid that unless Owen is on the Board to oppose me . . . the expenditure relative to the building will be curtailed." Henry did not bother to claim that such fears were unjustified, asserting instead that "in the long run the character of young Renwick will be found safer in my hands than those of Mr. Owen."[33]

The political maneuvering was not confined to Washington alone. Preston wrote on April 30 that he had "had the pleasure of a visit from Captain Wilkes." Somehow Wilkes had discovered that Preston's resignation was in Henry's hands, and the South Carolinian told him that he had made it subject to Henry's approval. Wilkes "expressed himself favourable to the reelection of Mr. Owen," but Preston's obvious disagreement had cut the conversation short. Preston held firm, as did Hawley, and the Library Committee came to the conclusion that the "absence of Mr. Rush is not a sufficient reason for leaving the Board." By late May Henry could write to Asa Gray that Owen "apparently acquiesces in the decision of the committee."[34]

Owen and Hough were out, and even though the appointment of Marsh had strengthened the book men, Henry hoped that he could gain control of the Institution in due time. The original regents, he noted, were "fast passing out, and those which remain are either my fast friends or take but little interest in the affair."[35] Put in an optimistic frame of mind by his victory over Owen, Henry would soon discover that the book men took more than a "little interest" in the Smithsonian.

His year and a half in Washington had taught Henry quite well how to cope with the political aspects of his position. In the midst of the controversy over Owen's reappointment, Henry's friend John Torrey described, or perhaps wishfully prescribed, the Secretary's new disposition. "I am glad that you have grown somewhat *pachydermatous*, so that little things no longer annoy you. Living for some time in Washington is said to produce such a happy change of the integuments. I must try a short residence there myself for my skin is entirely too thin for comfort."[36] Although little things may have ceased to annoy Henry, big things, especially big buildings, had not, and the Secretary turned his attention to the rising edifice.

Chapter Five

✕

PUBLIC ARCHITECTURE:
Hints and Hazards

SECRETARY Henry succeeded in forcing Robert Dale Owen off the Board of Regents, but he could not undo all that Owen had done. With the help of his brother, Owen had drawn up a prototypical plan for a Smithsonian Building, chosen an architect to adapt and implement that plan, and watched over its progress to the point where completion was inevitable. Owen remained on the Board long enough to make sure that the exterior of the building was set: Joseph Henry could not change a thing.

Exactly the opposite was true of the interior: Henry could and did change everything as permitted by the clause that Bache had inserted in the contract. Succeeding chapters will show that not one major room of the completed building performed the function that the Owen-Renwick plan originally assigned it. Henry gutted the entire main building, converted the east wing into offices and a residence, and transformed the west wing from art gallery to library.

Henry finally had control of the building, but Owen still had one more service to perform for the Institution. He was to write *Hints on Public Architecture* (fig. 23) through which the building committee explained their choice of the Norman style. The book was the most extensive forum for Owen's views on architecture, and also served as a subtle means of promotion of the career of young Renwick.

While Owen had the luxury of a hundred pages of text, Secretary Henry, who had taught short courses on architecture at Princeton

Figure 23. Title page, Hints on Public Architecture *by Robert Dale Owen (New York, 1849). Designed by James Renwick, Jr.*

and the Albany Academy, found only a limited expression, through passages in scientific papers and through an unfinished essay, "Thoughts on Architecture." Although Henry would have been loath to admit it, great similarities existed in their respective architectural theories. Both men believed that architecture must express the spirit of the age, that architecture must emulate Nature, and that the form of a building must be integrally related to its function. Both looked forward to the creation of a new style, but whereas Owen hoped for a style to emerge out of eclectic borrowing, Henry looked for a completely new style responsive to the physical characteristics of new materials such as iron and glass.

Robert Dale Owen, in *Hints on Public Architecture*, showed two very strong architectural preferences, one explicit, the other implicit. Most explicit was his preference for medieval architecture, Gothic and especially Norman, to the neoclassical styles. Somewhat less overt was his preference for James Renwick, Jr., to any other architect, Gothicist or Classicist, in the United States. In all likelihood this bias was inadvertent, but it nevertheless permeates the volume.

Owen wrote the text himself, but he received "considerable assistance from Mr. Renwick, in preparing drawings for woodcut illustrations, revising text, &c." Et cetera included introducing Owen to the vestrymen of Grace Church, and personally visiting the vestry of Trinity Church and the executives of A. T. Stewart & Company, all in hopes of persuading them to pay for plates of their buildings to appear in *Hints*. Owen hoped to feature two perspective views of the accepted Norman plan of Renwick, and one each of Renwick's Gothic plan, Haviland's Norman design, either Arnot or Notman's Gothic plan, and Daniels's "Italian" effort, as well as views of Girard College in Philadelphia, A. T. Stewart's Italianate dry-goods store, and Grace, Trinity, and Calvary churches in New York. The plates of losing competition entries were dependent on the architects' willingness to reduce their drawings to the needed size. Apparently none of the architects was willing, for the only unsuccessful entry published in *Hints* was Renwick's Gothic plan. Girard College was reduced to a three-inch woodcut, Richard Upjohn's Trinity was replaced by his Church of the Holy Communion, and the Italianate Stewart's dry-goods store did not appear at all. Twelve of the ninety-nine woodcuts depicted Renwick's work, and, more important, five of the six full-page lithographs and seven of the nine full-page wood engravings—eight of nine if the Renwick-drawn title page is included—were of Renwick buildings.[1]

In the fashion of the day, Owen did not identify the architects whose works he discussed; he did, however, deal extensively with Renwick's works. He referred to the neoclassicist Thomas U. Walter only because he had designed Girard College, Owen's foil throughout the volume. Owen's predilection for the medieval styles did not, however, lead him to discuss the works of its major practitioners. The works of such Renwick rivals as Richard Upjohn, Leopold Eidlitz, and Alexander Jackson Davis were barely mentioned. Owen also ignored the most prominent precedent in America for the use of Gothic for an educational structure: New York University by Town, Davis and Dakin. In *Hints on Public Architecture*, Owen seemed bent on proving that the Smithsonian Institution had engaged the services of the leading architect in America. Even Renwick, prideful as he was, must have known that it was excessive.

If Owen's treatment of contemporary architects and their work was narrow, his familiarity with recent works on medieval architecture was broad and impressive. He utilized such pioneering British studies as Thomas Rickman's *Attempt to Discriminate the Styles of English Architecture*, John Britton's *Cathedral Antiquities of England* and *Architectural Antiquities of Great Britain*, and Auguste Charles Pugin's *Specimens of the Architectural Antiquities of Normandy*. Two more recent sources exerted the greatest influence on Owen: Thomas Hope's *Historical Essay on Architecture*, which was posthumously published in 1835, and *The Architectural Magazine*, edited by John Claudius Loudon.[2]

Owen generously acknowledged the influence Hope's work had had on his own. He observed that he had "frequently fallen into the same train of thought which runs through Thomas Hope's well-known Historical Essay; than which few more valuable works on Architecture have ever appeared, in our own or in any other language." Hope had been a devoted neoclassicist, and had played a leading role in the controversy over the selection of a style for Downing College, Cambridge. He strongly disapproved of the Roman design by James Wyatt, then the most prominent architect in England, and offered as an alternative a Greek scheme by William Wilkins that was eventually adopted though only partially carried out. In

—

addition to taking part in such public debates and his private efforts to improve his town and country residences, Hope was a historian, and the *Historical Essay* was his most extensive work. Oddly enough, Hope spent a great deal of time discussing Lombard and Gothic architecture, including four chapters discussing the then-current controversy over which nation had originated the pointed arch. Through such detailed consideration of the medieval styles and through the extensive illustrations, which were collected in a second volume, Hope the neoclassicist influenced Ruskin and his generation, particularly with regard to the *Rundbogenstil*, the revival of rounded-arch architecture.[3]

Hope advocated borrowing from various historical styles whatever was useful, ornamental, scientific, or tasteful. He based this plea for an eclecticism of style merged with modern conveniences on the belief that such an architecture, "born in our country, grown on our soil, and in harmony with our habits, at once elegant, appropriate and original, shall truly deserve the appellation of 'our own.'" Owen quoted *verbatim* the concluding paragraph of the *Historical Essay* in the first chapter of *Hints*, and ended the book with the suggestion that the Smithsonian Building possessed "not a little of what may be fitting and appropriate in any manner, (should the genius of our country hereafter work such out,) that shall deserve to be named as a National Style of Architecture for America."[4]

Owen, like Hope, had no use for archaeological exactitude as an aesthetic criterion. He believed that "when the antiquary becomes the lawgiver . . . the knowledge which should serve to guide and to assist, may be perverted so as only to clog and hinder." Both men frankly expected the buildings of their time to incorporate modern innovations. Historical styles were to provide inspiration, but copying was out of the question: Owen and Hope expected modern buildings to surpass the old in convenience and in beauty, and they further expected this synthesis of old and new to give rise to a new style.[5]

Hope provided Owen with a historical perspective and a general notion of stylistic eclecticism, but Owen was eclectic not only in his architectural tastes but also in his architectural theory. His elaboration of the concept of "fitness" reflects the influence of John Claudius Loudon, and via Loudon the theory of associationism as formulated by the Scottish philosopher Archibald Alison. David Dale

Owen had consulted Loudon's *Architectural Magazine* in 1845 when
drawing up his plan for the Smithsonian, and his brother ordered a
set of the magazine for the Institution in November 1846. Although there are no textual references to Alison or Loudon—Owen
may have thought their specialties, aesthetics and residential architecture, off the subject of public architecture—the book cannot make
sense without an understanding of their theories.[6]

Alison and his colleagues adhered essentially to the empirical philosophy of John Locke. Concerning himself with the basic question
of how man comes to knowledge of the world, Locke denied the
Platonic belief that the human mind possessed ideas prior to experience. For Locke the mind was not a collection of innate ideas but
a "tabula rasa," a blank slate which recorded information received
from the outside world. Knowledge was the result of experience.

Locke's eighteenth-century followers realized that empiricism was
not without its difficulties. A philosophy based on sense impressions from the real world seemed to have little room for nonconcrete
ideas like "God" or "morality," and indeed David Hume developed
an empiricism profoundly skeptical of man's ability to know anything with certainty. On another level, Locke's image of the mind
as a blank slate did not allow for a mechanism to sort out the various
sense impressions pouring in. Somehow the mind had to be able to
give order to its newly acquired knowledge, but Locke's theory left
unclear just how this was done.

Scottish philosophers such as Dugald Stewart and Henry Home,
Lord Kames, known as "Common Sense Realists," modified Locke's
empiricism by arguing that the mind possessed certain "faculties"
that directed incoming sense impressions to the appropriate corner
of the mind. In addition to providing a mechanism for associating
like ideas within the mind, "faculty psychology" suggested that
man possesses a "moral sense," a faculty for discerning right from
wrong, which countered the pervasive skepticism of a David Hume.

Alison, a Scotsman well conversant with these ideas, applied them
to aesthetics in his *Essays on the Nature and Principles of Taste*. He
argued that beauty, far from being an attribute inherent in certain
objects and absent in others, was in the eye of the perceiver, or,
more precisely, in the ability of the mind to associate any given
sense impression with similar sensations previously perceived. Ali-

son claimed that feelings of beauty arose only when a building or a room is perceived to be fit for the task it performs. The beauty of an edifice could be evaluated not in abstract terms of ideal proportions but only in relative terms of how well it functioned and appeared to function. "Fitness" and the "expression of fitness" became the crucial aesthetic determinants.[7]

Alison's personal taste ran toward the classical, but his theory served to undermine the position of the classicists. The denial of the inherent beauty of symmetrical structures weakened the claim of the classical to preeminence, and the concept of fitness seemed to favor no particular style—and thus encouraged an eclectic point of view. Such eclecticism was furthered by the concept of historical associations. While the fitness of a building would impress experts in architecture, the memories of historical events conjured up by a given style would influence the aesthetic judgments of men of letters. Classical architecture contained many positive associations, but other styles were equally rich, and they were without the familiarity that lessened the impact of the classical on the viewer.

Alison's concepts remained at the theoretical level in his *Essays*. John Claudius Loudon applied those principles to the rural residential architecture of England in his *Encyclopaedia of Cottage, Farm, and Villa Architecture* (1833), and in the five volumes of *The Architectural Magazine*. For Loudon as for Alison, fitness was a central idea: Loudon saw the three most important factors in architecture as fitness, the expression of fitness, and the expression of style. Mere fitness, without the external expression of that fitness, was, Loudon contended, untruthful. Each house required some expression of its functional attributes, as well as an expression of style. Style, however, was essentially external, and lacked the integral relation of exterior and interior found in the expression of fitness.[8]

Loudon's work on rural residential architecture was of limited usefulness to Owen, who had no intention of becoming the Loudon of American public architecture. *Hints* was to be at once more theoretical and more historical than Loudon's work, and devoted to a different building type. Thus, Robert Dale Owen in *Hints on Public Architecture* achieved a synthesis of the associational theory of Alison and the historical approach of Hope. The result was a theory of architectural history in which buildings express the spirit of an age because "truthful" architecture expresses the internal functions of a building, and those functions in turn reflect the needs and aspirations of the civilization.

A true architecture, Owen argued, must "mould itself to the wants and domestic habits and the public customs and the political institutions and the religious sentiments of its day and age." This was not simply an architectural issue, but a moral one, for "truth" was the foundation of morality as of architecture. And truth, for Owen, was the expression of fitness. "External form should be the interpreter of internal purpose. That the interpretation be faithful is the first requisite; it is the province of genius, after that, to clothe it with grace and power"[9]—that is, to give it a historical style. Any style would do, so long as it possessed grace and power, but the expression of fitness was to be required of all styles.

The implication was that as civilization changed, architecture must change with it. No ancient form of beauty, when divorced from utility, was appropriate for the nineteenth century. "To retain a form, no matter how graceful its outline or ornamental its parts, in utter disconnection from the true and original purpose which first suggested it, is like clinging to the lifeless corpse after the spirit which animated it has passed away."[10] Architecture, like civilization itself, was for Owen vital, changing, evolving: in a word, organic.

The Greek Revival, Owen contended, was inappropriate because the needs and aspirations of the nineteenth century clashed with those of classical times, and especially because the Greek temple form was too inflexible to be functional or to properly express fitness. "Our domestic habits, our public customs, our religious exercises, are all wholly different from those of the Greeks," he noted. As an example of the difficulty of expressing fitness with a Greek temple, Owen offered the problem of chimneys, for which the ancients had no need. "In the language of the classical architect, a chimney is a sordid subject," Owen chided. The classicist "regrets its necessity, and tasks his ingenuity to mask and conceal its existence, as a blemish in his plan." He compared such a lack of truthfulness to the Gothic style, where the "evidence of warmth within, the chimney, not only ceases to be a blemish, but becomes ornamental."[11]

The verdict was essentially the same for both classical Roman and Renaissance architecture. Owen approvingly quoted Thomas Hope, who insisted that if the Romans had had any taste or imagination, they would have used their technological innovation, the arch, as the basis for "some new species of ornamental addition, appearing to belong to its nature and composition." Again, the expression of function was the issue, for the Romans, according to Owen, hid their arches from view by covering them "with a Grecian mask." Such practices of the Romans and their later admirers possessed "no unity, no truth, no intrinsic integrity, and therefore no elements of permanence, no living energy. . . . It is based upon false appearances and cannot endure." Owen believed that this falsehood offended both utility and taste, because "even the uncultivated eye finds pleasure in the display of constructive relations. When a noble task is achieved, it pleases us to perceive, at a glance, how it is done."[12] Beauty, then, was the perception of fitness.

Medieval architecture was singled out for its expression of constructive relations. "I like its truth, its candor, its boldness," Owen wrote. "I like its lofty character, its aspiring lines, I like the independence with which it has shaken off the shackles of formal rule, and refused obedience to the despotic laws of monotonous repetition. I like its changeful aspects, the infinite succession of its forms, the endless variety of character in its expressions." The irregular variety of the Gothic style was not simply picturesque, Owen claimed, but also utilitarian, since towers and wings could be added without ruining the outline of the building; indeed, the additions might heighten the picturesque effect. In this quest for variety, man was merely following the example of Nature. "No leaf in the forest . . . is a servile copy of its fellow," Owen asserted. While man could not be expected to achieve the infinite variety of Nature in human endeavors, neither should he expend his energies in attempting to depart from her example. To Owen, then, medieval architecture was both truthful and attuned to Nature.[13]

In Owen's eyes, however, later Gothic had become too florid and excessively ornate. The earlier, bolder, and simpler Norman style laid claim to special virtues. "It exhibits more mass and breadth than the true Gothic," Owen suggested; "it had more of simplicity and severity of outline; it is less cut up with adventitious and ambitious ornament; altogether, it has less air of pretension and more appearance of solidity." Without making an absolute choice between the Norman and the Gothic, he nevertheless suggested that the late

Norman and the early Gothic styles were most responsive to internal functions and thus to the needs of the civilization. The Smithsonian Building provided a good example of this, since the ground plan "was, in substance, determined, before even the style of Architecture was fixed upon. . . . Yet I do not think it wanting in harmony or general effect." [14]

At the same time, the Norman style called up associations appropriate to the Smithsonian. Owen did not "believe that any one, of moderately cultivated taste, in looking upon that building, would mistake its character, or connect it, in his mind, with other than a scientific or collegiate foundation." In addition to such general associations, Owen claimed that the two wings of the building were "intelligibly stamped with the general character of object for which they are, respectively, designed: the east wing . . . set apart for the severer sciences, as Chemistry and Natural Philosophy, hinting by its somewhat solid and massive outline, at gravity of purpose; while the west wing, intended to contain a Gallery of Art, intimates, by its lighter proportions and airier forms, the spirit, more of grace and ornament, of its destination." [15]

Owen contended, as had Archibald Alison, that historical associations might draw the attention of viewers away from the expression of fitness. "We ought to be upon our guard," Owen claimed, "against the influence which the power of association involuntarily exerts upon the mind." Associations might tempt the architect to copy beautiful buildings of past ages, regardless of their fitness for modern use. "Beauty is, in a measure, a relative quality," he wrote. "Strike from beauty its propriety, its fitness; let it become unsuitable and unmeaning, and its essence is gone; a showy but worthless mask alone remains." [16] The Norman and Gothic styles avoided such unsuitability, Owen contended, because their most picturesque features were also expressions of fitness.

Even so, Owen did not remain consistent in his treatment of associationism. When arguing against the exact imitation of any historical style, he was capable of providing the darker associations of the medieval style. Americans who admire the "castellated heights" on the Rhine, he wrote, the "dark masses and picturesque outline" of which added so much "to the romantic beauty of that noble stream," should not regret the lack of such sights in their native country.

Figure 24. Smithsonian Building. View from the northeast. Photography by A. J. Russell, ca. 1862.

Those visitors should instead "call to mind, that these lordly castles, with all their poetical accessories of moat and bastions, of battlement and tower, were once but the strongholds of titled robbers, the receptacles of plunder, the scenes of extortion and cruelty and rapine."[17]

By Owen's own admission, then, a Norman castle (fig. 24) could inspire thoughts of either a collegiate foundation or a receptacle of plunder. Whatever the appropriateness of these may seem for a public building at Washington, such associations were but a corollary of Owen's main contention. At the core of his theory remained the expression of fitness, and it was this idea that informed nearly every page of *Hints on Public Architecture*.

The only extensive review of the volume, in *The Literary World* of New York, was highly critical, though it referred to the architect of the Smithsonian Building as a "skillful expositor" of the Norman style, and to the building itself as a "very fair sample of all the shades and varieties of that style of art." The author, Robert Carey Long, Jr., was a Baltimore architect recently removed to New York. Long praised Owen's advocacy of "Truthfulness," but insisted that "Truth in Architecture stops not merely with general expression of purpose and harmony of outward and inward division." He then proceeded to take Owen to task on a variety of points large and small.[18]

Long offered as a "specimen of pure twaddle" Owen's statement that Americans should not envy those castles on the Rhine since they had housed titled robbers. "Yet it is from these very castles," observed Long, "these hindrances to the happiness of the million, these democratic abominations, that the accessories of bastion and battlement in the Smithsonian building have been most largely drawn by this identical chairman."

Concerning Owen's recommendation of the Norman as an inexpensive style, because the stone need not be smoothly cut, Long denied both the principle and the application. "This cheapness, this desire of producing the most show at the least cost, is the bane of Modern Architecture." As to the cost of smooth versus rusticated stone, Long pointed out that roughly cut stone was used not only by medieval architects but also by architects of the Italian Renaissance. "Did Mr. Owen never see or hear of the Pitti Palace?"

In comparing the "functional" buttresses of the Smithsonian Building with "ornamental" pilasters on Greek Revival structures, Owen had made the mistake of citing as his example the Customs House in New York by Town, Davis and Dakin. Long was quick to point out that the pilasters—actually square piers—on the Customs House were load-bearing, and that the "intervening wall might be entirely removed without destruction to the edifice. . . . The wall is but a mere filling-in screen."

Long's defense of the Greek Revival was based almost entirely on Town, Davis and Dakin's Customs House, one of the most innovative designs of the period. Even Long, however, could not bring himself to defend Girard College. "Now, we are no admirers of this

Figure 25. Joseph Henry.

building; on the contrary we consider it a dead failure, a perfect impropriety, the worst kind of mistake, a well-builded one. But it must be remembered that it was designed during the Greco-mania period, and its total inapplicability is the fault of its day." Long was not so willing to tolerate Owen's enthusiasm for the Norman style, finding that the "architectural devotion of the Chairman of the Building Committee of the Institute has passed into the phase of monomania—indeed a very full moon Norman lunacy."

Joseph Henry (fig. 25) who more than two years before had come to the conclusion that Owen was "struck with an architectural mania," might have taken some grim satisfaction from Long's scathing review. He continued to believe that the "architecture of the 12th century is not well adapted to the wants of the 19th." He rejected both eclectic borrowing from or archaeological duplication of historical styles. Nevertheless, Henry agreed—in principle, at least—with Owen that form could not be determined until the precise functions of the organization to be housed were known, and that architecture reflects the spirit of an age. But Henry insisted that a new style for a new age would have to evolve out of new materials such as iron and glass; he particularly admired the Crystal Palace in London. [19]

Henry considered the buildings of a country and age to be "ethnological expressions of the wants, habits, arts, and feelings of the time in which they were erected." Through their monuments, Egypt, Greece, and Rome "sought to convey to future ages an idea of their religious and political sentiments." He strongly urged the preservation of the architecture of past epochs while denying their appropriateness for the nineteenth century. "Every vestige of ancient architecture which now remains on the face of the earth should be preserved with religious care; but to servilely copy these, and to attempt to apply them to the uses of our day, is as preposterous as to endeavor to harmonize the refinement and civilization of the present age with the superstition and barbarity of the times of the Pharaohs." So deeply did Henry believe that art and architecture reflect the spirit of their times that it became for him an aesthetic imperative. "It is only when a building expresses the dominant sentiment of an age, when a perfect adaptation to its use is joined to harmony of proportions and an outward expression of its character, that it is entitled to our admiration." [20] In his concern for the expression of an individual building's character as well as the sentiment of the age, Henry virtually echoed Owen's argument.

Like Owen, Henry admired the original Greek temples and denied their usefulness in a modern world. For the architect of the Greek temple, Henry wrote, the mission was not utilitarian, as with modern building, but aesthetic, because the temple was built to gratify the deity. "Its minutest parts were exquisitely finished, since nothing but perfection on all sides and in the smallest particulars could satisfy an all-seeing and critical eye." However, since the edifice was the focal point in an outdoor ceremony rather than a hall in which worshippers gathered, the temple was built without concern for heating or ventilation. Henry therefore agreed with Owen that the "uses . . . to which buildings of this kind can be applied in modern times are exceedingly few. . . . They cannot be copied in our day without violating the principles which should govern architectural adaptation."

Henry attributed such unwise borrowing from historical styles to the "desire for individual aggrandizement" exacerbated by American institutions, which tended to break down social distinctions. "In our desire to signalize ourselves individually we seize on any circumstance which may separate us from the mass—we are delighted with an opportunity of exhibiting our superiority particularly in those things in which the common herd can have no cultivation." Revivalism was also encouraged by American colleges, which stressed "literary" rather than "intellectual" pursuits. "Any thing therefore which is in the remotest degree connected with the exclusiveness of the past rather than with the vulgarism of the present finds prejudice in the conventionally learned mind in its favor." A prime example of this, in Henry's eyes, was Girard College, a "beautiful copy of a Greek temple but which is utterly useless as a modern schoolhouse." The need for lighting and ventilation brought windows and chimneys to the classical façade, "and in the end we have a hybrid, neither hawk nor buzzard."[21]

For Henry, Girard College because of its great expense was an ominous foreshadowing of what might happen to the Smithsonian bequest. In a draft of his essay "Thoughts on Architecture," Henry followed his discussion of Girard College by flatly stating that "another example which will stand as a lasting memento of bad taste, of stupid interference to render the funds of a noble bequest worse than abortive, which will serve to perpetuate the same error unless the evil be exposed and commented upon, is the Smithsonian building." Henry had nothing against the original castles on the Rhine; indeed, he admired them because "every part is in keeping with the ideas and strategy of feudal warfare." To the Secretary, Norman castles were no more adaptable to the nineteenth century than Greek temples were, for the Smithsonian Building was merely one "of our modern pasteboard edifices, in which, with their battlements, towers, pinnacles, 'fretted roofs and long drawn aisles,' cheap and transient magnificence is produced by painted wood or decorated plaster."[22] Indeed, Owen had attacked the use of plaster on Greek temples as "untruthful" but failed to mention its extensive use on the Smithsonian Building as well as on other works of James Renwick, Jr.

Owen had argued that the Smithsonian Building expressed its fitness because the external form had been based on a previously drawn ground plan, but Henry insisted that Owen's ground plan was not an accurate reflection of the needs of the Institution. "The first point to be settled, in commencing building, is the uses to which it is to be applied," Henry explained in the *Tenth Annual Report of the Smithsonian.* "This, however, could not be definitely ascertained at the beginning of the Institution, and hence the next wisest step to that of not commencing to build immediately, was to defer the completion of the structure until the plan of operations and the wants of the establishment were more precisely known." [23] With characteristic optimism, Owen had assumed more than a year before his Smithsonian bill passed that his agenda for the Institution would ultimately be carried out. The plan of David Dale Owen had anticipated all sorts of functions, but it had not anticipated Joseph Henry.

Both Robert Dale Owen and Henry turned to nature to justify their description of architecture as adaptive and evolving. But whereas Owen had stressed the endless variety of flowers in picturesque array, Henry stressed the manner in which animals, human and otherwise, adapted their housing to fit their needs. "It is surely better," Henry observed, "to imitate the example of the mollusc, who, in fashioning his shell, adapts it to the form in dimensions of his body, rather than that of another animal who forces himself into a house intended for a different occupant." Setting aside the pre-Darwinian assertion that the mollusc has the power to adapt its shell to its need, Henry clearly believed that form can only be determined in relation to the needs of the intended occupant.

If Henry was sympathetic to the idea of expression of fitness, he had no use for historical associations. The "conventionally learned mind" might place greater value on the past than the present, but Henry insisted on the necessity of a new architecture. As for the association of the west wing of the Smithsonian Building with art and the east wing with science, what was "intelligibly stamped" for Owen was not for Henry. A year before *Hints* appeared, he wrote that the west wing "will be very handsome." The east wing, home of science and, eventually, his family, he did not like, either on the interior or the exterior. The difference to Henry was not art versus science, but beauty versus ugliness.[24]

Having rejected the historical styles as a source for a new style of architecture, Henry pointed to several factors that such a new architecture would have to take into account. Architecture, he believed, "should change not only with the character of the people, and in some cases with the climate, but also with the material to be employed in construction." Owen had briefly mentioned the potential of iron early in *Hints on Public Architecture*, but Henry pressed on to claim that the "use of iron and glass requires an entirely different style from that which sprung from the rocks of Egypt, the masses of marble with which the lintels of the Grecian temples were formed, or the introduction of brick by the Romans." This new style could take advantage of the "great tenacity of iron, and its power of resistance to crushing," which would result in a "far more slender and apparently lighter arrangement of parts." Henry had personally observed the more frequent use of cast iron during his trip to Great Britain in 1837. To his fellow scientist Michael Faraday he wrote in 1851, "I consider the Crystal Palace [fig. 26] the true architectural exponent of the feelings and wants of the present day." Designed by Sir Joseph Paxton and the engineers Fox and Henderson, the glass and iron Crystal Palace covered under one roof almost nineteen acres of the Great Exhibition of the Works of Industry of All Nations. Secretary Henry's admiring comment on the building came just one month after Queen Victoria officially opened the exhibition on May 1, 1851.[25]

Ironically, both Robert Dale Owen and Joseph Henry endorsed the idea of expression of fitness and its corollary, Truthfulness in architecture. By encouraging a belief that beauty was relative to function, the same idea led Owen and Henry to diametrically opposed conclusions. For Owen Truth was in a flexible and picturesque building, drawn from a variety of historical sources and unconcerned about an occasional plaster column. *Hints on Public Architecture* foretold the increasing eclecticism of the later nineteenth century. To Henry, iron or wood plastered over to resemble a column was the height of untruthfulness. His insistence on the truthful expression of material and his advocacy of new materials placed Henry in the avant-garde of mid-nineteenth century architectural thinkers.

Figure 26. Sir Joseph Paxton, Fox & Henderson Engineers, The Crystal Palace, London. 1850–1851.

Robert Dale Owen had praised the fitness of the Smithsonian Building, claiming that any adaptations or additions to the building could only increase its picturesque effect. This was little consolation to Joseph Henry, because no matter how extensive the adaptations were, they would have to be in the Norman style. Nevertheless, Henry set to work at shaping the interior of the building to meet the needs of his Institution.

Chapter Six

". . . NOT TO BE TRUSTED"

WHEN the five-year contract of James Renwick, Jr., expired in 1852, the exterior of the Smithsonian Building was completed, as were the interiors of the two wings and the two ranges, but the interior of the main building was little more than what Joseph Henry later called a "forest of timber." So numerous were the difficulties, large and small, on the building site that Renwick left under a cloud of suspicion. In fact, Henry's mistrust of the architect had been growing for several years.[1]

As early as March 1848, James Renwick, Jr. (fig. 27) assured Joseph Henry that the east wing, with its chemical lecture room and laboratories, would be ready to be occupied by the end of the summer, and that the west wing would be completed by the end of the year. Henry, when relaying this information to Charles Coffin Jewett, added a proviso: "or at least this is the intention of the architect, and from what has been done I presume it will be accomplished." Henry was clearly somewhat suspicious of the architect's schedule.[2]

The calm that followed the storm over Owen engendered an optimistic outlook on Henry's part. In May 1848 he wrote that "all things relative to the Smithsonian in Congress are just now very quiet and the prospect of usefulness and permanency of the Institution I think becoming every day more favourable. The building is going on quite rapidly and will be ready for use according to the last account of the architect in about three months." The Secretary confided to Asa Gray that he was at last resigned to seeing the

Figure 27. James Renwick, Jr., holding plans for his next great project, St. Patrick's Cathedral, New York. Oil portrait by John W. Ehringer. 1853.

building going up. "I have concluded not to attempt to stop the erection, but to endeavor to control the expenditure."[3] Having recognized that completion of the building was inevitable, Henry turned to the task of minimizing costs and adapting the interior of the building to his own plans.

To that end Henry began seeing more of young Renwick, even while Owen was still coming to the construction site and directing the work. The Secretary paid particular attention to the east wing and range, which, under the Owen plan, contained a chemical lecture room and smaller rooms for chemical apparatus and for students. In late May, Henry gave the architect the plans of cases for the scientific equipment. Recalling Owen's original agenda for the Institution, Henry wryly commented to Bache that the Smithsonian "is not at present to be converted into a normal school, and as we will want much more room for apparatus than we can obtain until the main building is finished I have suggested the propriety of devoting the room called the student's laboratory to apparatus." Henry had already procured so many items that the yet-to-be-completed east wing could "scarcely more than contain" them.[4]

Henry continued to redesign the interior space in accordance with his own designs for the Institution. The poor lighting in the laboratories south of the lecture room in the east wing elicited sarcasm from the Secretary. "The perfection of architecture, the Norman style, has furnished a laboratory in the rear of the small lecture room which may be sufficiently lighted with several gas burners on a cloudy day." The problem was a partition which created a small room or a large closet against the south wall, and which also blocked the southern exposure. The laboratories themselves received the light from two-thirds of a rounded-head window, on the east and west walls, against which the partition abutted (see fig. 14). Rather than simply remove the partition, Henry's solution was to place glass windows in the partition "so as to give it more light from the adjoining rooms—this will be done."

The Secretary found Renwick to be "exceedingly obliging" and "disposed to make any changes" Henry suggested. It appeared to Henry, however, that the "architect did not understand the plan of the small lecture room," and had run timber for the gallery on three sides, blocking off the light from the windows at the northern end of the room, the planned rear of the hall. Observed Henry, "the plan of Mr. Owen is that of a gallery on either side and the graded rising of the seats to . . . the gallery in the rear. This plan will be better for light but I am not yet sure of the esthetic effect. Utility, however, before beauty is my maxim."

The Secretary was resolved not only to offer constructive criticisms on the site but to influence policy decisions at the source. "I intend to be present hereafter at all meetings of the building committee whether I am asked or not and to have an eye on all that is going on." By August, however, Henry's hard-won autonomy began to seem less desirable, as Renwick urged the Secretary to allow him to "push the work during the present good weather," assuring him that the expenditure would not be excessive. Such decisions gave

Henry "uneasiness every time I think of them." He once again turned to Bache for advice. Renwick promised to stay within the range of $41,000 for construction costs for the year 1848. "Should not I insist on an inspection of the accounts? Does Colonel Totten know anything about the financial matters?"[5]

Henry's budding mistrust of the architect may well have been fueled by a petition which over twenty local builders presented to the Congress in June of 1848. The petition alleged that inferior timber was being used on the Smithsonian Building, timber acquired at a price half of that stipulated in the contract. After listing several other complaints, the builders warned that if the rest of the edifice were built by such standards, "it will become in less than fifty years *hence*, a tottering *rotten dilapidated wreck*, a *disgrace* to the age." Both the contractor, Gilbert Cameron, and the carpenter, John Sniffen, had worked on other Renwick buildings in New York. The architect was not responsible for their alleged violations of the contract, but such accusations could not have been comforting to Henry as he pondered how much trust he could place in the architect.[6]

Nevertheless, Joseph Henry had his own dreams of what the building could be, and the role it would perform in his Institution. After the completion of the main building, with its intended larger lecture room on the first floor, he hoped to throw the entire east wing "into one room with a gallery around it and a large table in the middle for the use of the savants which may be annually assembled for the discussion of scientific subjects." The room would be transformed from a lecture hall into a gigantic seminar room for the use of the leading intellectuals of the day. As always, Henry looked to enhance facilities for the increase of knowledge; every college and school in the country had some sort of lecture room, but Henry's Smithsonian was to be an international clearinghouse and meeting place for those involved in advanced research. He wrote to Bache that this plan was a "scheme for the future," but he broached the subject with Renwick as well, and even received an estimate that for $600 the alterations could be done. All this came months before the east wing was completed.[7]

Renwick had promised to have the east wing ready by summer's end. That goal was not met, but the building committee was able to report by the end of 1848 that the wing lacked only the cases to be installed for apparatus. The west wing's exterior was also finished, and the foundation of the main building had been laid. The campanile and octagonal towers and the two smaller corner towers of the main building jutted up 30 feet from the ground. Despite the delay in finishing the east wing, the building committee remained optimistic that the entire building would be completed by March 1852, the originally planned date.[8]

By May 1849 Joseph Henry was able to move his office into the building. For over a year he had been ensconced in a small room at the Patent Office, where he was uncomfortably close to the collections of the Wilkes expedition, which he feared—rightly—the Smithsonian would have to accept for the National Museum. Once in the Castle, he appropriated as offices two rooms over the laboratories on the south side of the east wing. These were the only upper-story rooms in the east wing; the chemical lecture room with its galleries had an especially high ceiling, and the story-and-a-half east range had only what Henry called "cubbies." Apparently the Owen-Renwick plan did not anticipate having to heat the two rooms on what Owen had referred to as the "mezzanine story," for Henry claimed in May that the rooms "have been very uncomfortable during the past week. The furnaces give scarcely any heat in our rooms, above the Laboratory."[9]

So it was with chilled fingers that Henry wrote to Bache concerning his new plan for the chemical lecture room. Soon after its completion, the room, which seated from three to four hundred persons, proved to be "entirely too small." Henry decided to remove the laboratory and apparatus rooms, thus creating one large room out of the whole wing, with seats for a thousand persons. He instructed Renwick to draw up plans, and later in May, the architect submitted several alternative plans to General Totten, who "chose the one with the oratory on the side," near the door to the east range. The arrangement placed the "apparatus rooms in the east connecting range . . . in close proximity with the lecturer's table," and seated as many people as the originally planned principal lecture room.[10]

A large lecture room in the east wing obviated the need for the originally intended lecture room in the main building, and opened up half of the space on the first floor, which had been evenly divided between the "Principal Lecture Room" and the library. Henry now proposed to devote part of the space to scientific equipment, and the rest to the library. A room measuring 65 feet by 50 at the east end of the first floor of the main building would serve as a "depository for physical apparatus." The remaining 35 feet × 50 was added to the library. In addition, Henry did away with the pair of large staircases at the north entrance and placed a single stairway in one of the north towers, thus opening up even more space for the library. Wrote Henry, "by these changes the capacity of the library has been increased upwards of one third." In these architectural decisions the Secretary demonstrated his willingness to cooperate fully with the book men.

All the changes were made, moreover, "without increasing the expense of the building." Henry even speculated that the contractor was "a gainer by alterations." He also suspected, however, that Renwick was attempting some gains on his own. "I am convinced by the course of the architect in relation to this business, that he is not to be trusted." Renwick had originally estimated that the new plan for the lecture room would cost another several hundred dollars. Henry responded that he "would have nothing to do with the change if there was any extra expense to it." Later that evening the Secretary was informed that the contractor had been willing all along to make the changes at no additional cost.

Renwick's high opinion of himself had also grated on Henry, as it had on the architect's old classmate, George Templeton Strong. In the presence of General Totten, Renwick "affected to know all about" the curve of sight in the lecture room, which Bache had explained to him, and Henry presumed that he "would have given it as his own, had I not been present." Whether the confusion was an honest mistake or a deliberate deception, mistrust between the architect and the Secretary was increasing.

Henry's constant suggestions and criticism led Renwick to defend himself by reminding the Secretary that all of the architects in the competition had provided exteriors to cover a floor plan already drawn up by the Owen brothers. This fact was news to Henry. "It appears that all the interior of the building was planned by Mr. Owen and his brother," he wrote in amazement to Senator James A. Pearce. "The architect excuses himself by insisting that the interior of the building is not his." Henry claimed that he felt "some hesitation at first in urging these changes on the building committee knowing that by so doing I incurred considerable responsibility," but he was convinced that the changes were for the best and was encouraged by General Totten's agreement as to their necessity. And since Henry "had opposed the adoption of so extensive a building, I was not much consulted as to the arrangements of the interior and, indeed they had all been settled in New Harmony before the plan of organization of the Institution was adopted." Although the building was not, he wrote, "what it might have been in the way of adaptation, still it will now be tolerably convenient and will certainly make a very imposing appearance." [11]

As the building progressed, the time to bring the library and museum into operation drew near. Toward those ends Henry acquired a large number of books for the library, and began the process of choosing an assistant for the museum. The books were those of George Perkins Marsh, one of the regents from the House, who was appointed Minister Resident to Turkey by President Zachary Taylor. As Marsh had recently lost much of his family fortune, the only way to finance his ministry in Turkey was to sell part of his beloved personal library. When the Smithsonian bought some $3000 worth of books, the grateful Marsh told Henry that he had "exacted a promise from his successor in Congress that he would watch over the interest of the Coast Survey, the Southern Astronomical Expedition and the Smithsonian Institution." The books were deposited in the west wing, which was intended to serve as the library until the completion of the main building. [12]

Henry and Marsh also had a candidate in mind for the position of assistant secretary for the museum. He was Spencer F. Baird, a naturalist at Dickinson College, who had first inquired about the possibility of employment with the Smithsonian in 1847. Henry was impressed with Baird, whom he thought would be "not a mere curator of a museum" but an original investigator. As always, Henry valued active research more than the diffusion of knowledge. This was fine with the book men, as long as an extensive library was part of the bargain, and both Marsh and Rufus Choate favored Baird's appointment. Another year was to pass before Henry, in July 1850, appointed Baird to "take charge of the museum and aid in the publications, &c." Unlike Jewett, who was nominated directly by Henry and appointed by the regents, Baird was appointed by the Secretary, a distinction which would become important later. [13]

By the end of 1849, the walls of the main building were up and the roof was in place, though the towers rose no higher than the top of the walls. Two months later, on February 26, 1850, Henry had just left the grounds when a "portion of the interior framing and floors of part of the main building, intended to contain the museum of apparatus, fell down into the basement." The Secretary immediately had that section of the building closed off, with orders to preserve the area until the architect could see it for himself. He then wrote a terse letter to Renwick, "requiring his immediate attendance." The architect, who was at home in New York City, reached Washington less than forty-eight hours after the accident. Henry, Renwick, and the building committee examined the part of the building where the timber had fallen through. The committee requested reports from the architect, the superintendent, and the contractor. They reported to the Board of Regents on the second of March.[14]

Apparently the regents were not satisfied with the accounts they received. They created a committee consisting of the members of the building committee—Jefferson Davis, Seaton, and Hilliard—Henry, Totten, and Bache, and "some competent and entirely impartial architect or architects" for the purpose of making a "survey of the whole building," to determine the extent of any contractual violations and to estimate the cost of repairing the damage. The special committee called in three architects: Colonel William Turnbull of the U.S. Topographical Engineers, Edward B. White of Charleston, South Carolina, and John R. Niernsee of Baltimore.

On April 20 the Regents heard the report of the committee, and also listened to Renwick's position. They decided to recommit the report "for such further action as may be deemed necessary," and, more threateningly, that "the Building Committee be directed to take legal advice as to the power possessed by the Regents, under the contract, and the course to be pursued should it be found necessary to declare it void; and that notice thereof be given to the contractor." Things were beginning to look ominous for Renwick and the subcontractors. On the very day that Renwick was defending the building and his men before the regents, the noted botanist John Torrey of New York wrote to Henry that he had "feared all along that young R. was incompetent. He has some talent in certain departments of architecture," Torrey admitted, "but lacks judgement and combining powers. He is also weak and easily imposed upon." Whatever the merits of Torrey's architectural criticism, he sharply underestimated the tenacity of the young architect, who was by no means ready to give up the Smithsonian project.[15]

Secretary Henry presented the final report of the special committee to the Board of Regents on July 3, 1850. The committee concluded that the "workmanship of the cut-stone of the exterior is good, and the masonry generally, though in some respects not of the best quality, is of a passable character with reference to the terms of the contract." The interior of the main building, however, was found to be "defective in the kind of materials originally adopted, and to a considerable degree in the quality of materials employed." In particular, the widespread use of wood was not proper "for a building intended to contain valuable deposits, many of which will be donations to the institution, presented with the implied condition that they are to be properly secured against danger from fire." The committee suggested that all existing interior work be removed, and that it be replaced with fireproof materials. This would add another $44,000 to the cost of the building, for a total of some $253,000.[16]

Renwick worked with the special committee in his dual role of architect and arbiter in disputes between the regents and the contractor. He devised a plan for a fireproof interior to the satisfaction of the committee, and drew up his own version of the cost of the building. His figure came to $245,000, which, he claimed, was "due to various deductions he has made on account of defective materials, imperfect workmanship, and changes in the plan." The deductions against the account of the contractor, Gilbert Cameron, seemed to penalize the shoddy work, but Renwick had subtly shifted the terms of the contract at the same time, so that Cameron was excused from certain contractual obligations. The original contract had been quite explicit that the contractor would not only finish the interior but also provide a substantial part of the furniture, from glass cases for the museum to seats for the lecture room to water closets. Renwick made it appear that he was being strict with Cameron and saving the regents $8,000 when much of the savings actually came from reducing the specifications in the contract. The regents must have been aware of this, but probably reasoned that

Figure 28. James Renwick, Jr., Trinity Episcopal Church, Washington, D.C. 1849. Photograph ca. 1864.

reducing Cameron's participation in the project was a positive de-velopment. On the motion of Senator Pearce, the board approved the report of the special committee. The decision to rebuild the whole interior made it less likely that the building would be com-pleted within the five years of the contract.

Renwick, meanwhile, was busily expanding his Washington con-nections. Several commissions came his way from the Washington banker William Wilson Corcoran. One, Trinity Episcopal Church (fig. 28) was built on land which Corcoran donated to the church,

at Third and C Streets, N.W. The design was adapted from Renwick's Gothic plan for the Smithsonian, with the wings cut off (cf.
figs. 28, 17). Renwick remodeled Corcoran's home on Lafayette
Square, adding two wings as well, and designed a small chapel and
the two massive entrance gates for Oak Hill Cemetery in Georgetown, for which Corcoran had purchased and donated the land. The
banker may have even confided to Renwick that he had plans to
erect a separate private art gallery to hold his large collection of
paintings and sculpture. That and the possibility of additional public patronage must have made the New Yorker feel no anxiety about
the delay at the Smithsonian Building.[17]

Work resumed, and the exterior of the building was completed
by the end of 1851. The building committee reported that the "majority of strangers who visit the city consider it a very beautiful
edifice, of which the effect will be heightened by the improvement
of the grounds and the planting of trees." Work still continued on
the superstructure of the interior, but was not far enough along to
require a decision on the arrangement of rooms. As late as February
1852, Henry was reminding the regents that Cameron's contract
was up on March 19, and that they had yet to decide about further
fireproofing and whether or not to build a larger lecture room in the
main building to replace the one in the east wing. The board referred the matter to the building committee, which reported back
on March 1 with a suggestion that the completion of the building
be pursued "as far as the funds will allow, and as rapidly as is consistent with good workmanship." No action was taken, however,
and on March 22, three days after the expiration date of the contract, the building committee "informed the Board that the work
on the building by the present contractor was not quite completed,
but might be expected to be so in about ten days." Cameron's des-
ignation as the "present" contractor had an ominous ring to it,
strongly hinting that he would not be allowed to see the building
to completion.[18]

The ten days necessary to meet the contractual obligations dragged
on through the spring and into the summer until July 12, when
Henry wrote to Renwick, telling him "to come on and make final
settlement with Cameron." The architect made the trip to Washington in late July, and informed Cameron that "it would take him two

or three weeks to make up the amount." Renwick left town on July 29, taking "with him all the plans which Cameron had in his possession." In early August, the architect wrote from New York that the "building, so far as it was embraced in the contract of Mr. Cameron, was completed," but he also requested several more days in which to calculate the final award.[19]

On August 6, Henry received another communication from Renwick, "demanding," as the Secretary put it in his diary, "payment from the Board for services since the end of the contract." Henry hastened to see Captain Charles Wilkes, Renwick's uncle, warning him that the letter "would produce bad results." Wilkes sent a note the next day, to say that he had consulted with the architect's younger brother, Edward, who then lived in Washington while working as an expert on patents. Edward claimed that he "had no authority to withhold the letter from its destination." Henry presented the letter to the regents at their meeting that evening. The building committee stated that they did not consider "themselves authorized to pay without an order from the Board." Graham Fitch of the committee then offered a resolution "relative to the accounts on Mr. Renwick," but action was postponed until the next meeting.[20]

The Board of Regents decided on August 9 that they would not wait any longer for the final calculations of Renwick. They empowered the building committee "to settle the accounts of Mr. Cameron, pursuant to his contract," unless the committee deemed it more prudent to "pay the money into court," for Cameron was currently being sued by John Sniffin, the subcontractor for carpentry. As for Renwick himself, Fitch's resolution of the last meeting was taken up and amended by General Totten; it was ordered that "Mr. Renwick, having reported by letter to the Building Committee that the Smithsonian building is completed, be notified that his services are no longer required by the Regents of this institution." The bills that the architect had presented for the spring and summer were to be paid only after he handed the regents the final certificate of the "completion" of the building.

So, all sides winked and agreed that the building, with its wooden superstructure and some fireproofing in place, but without a single room in the main building ready for occupation, was in fact complete. The strange maneuver freed Henry from Renwick, and, presumably, Cameron. Construction halted while Captain Barton S. Alexander, a Totten protégé from the Army Corps of Engineers, prepared "detailed drawings and plans for rendering the remainder of the building entirely fireproof." If Alexander's plan met the approval of the Board of Regents, they would allow him to superintend the project to completion.[21]

Chapter Seven

THE BATTLE OF THE WEST WING

A T the start of 1853, the Smithsonian Building consisted of two wings and two ranges flanking an empty shell. By the time the interior of the building was finally completed in 1855, Joseph Henry and his new architect, Captain Barton S. Alexander (fig. 29) had filled the shell of the main building with a museum on the first floor, and an apparatus room, a gallery of art, and a new lecture room on the second floor. In addition, they transformed the lecture room and laboratories of the east wing into the offices of the Institution, and, on a newly added second floor, a residence for the Secretary. Henry changed nothing in the arrangement of the library in the west wing, but he did topple the library from its place in the power structure of the Institution. In 1853, Henry controlled the east wing and the main building; in 1855, he controlled the entire Institution, and moved his family into the Castle.

With the departure of Renwick, the regents at first assumed that the contractor, Gilbert Cameron, had been disinvited as well. But on January 28, 1853, they received a letter from Cameron, alleging that his reputation as a builder would be injured unless he were allowed to complete the building. Some regents probably thought that his reputation was fixed either way, but the matter was referred to the building committee, which in turn referred it to J. M. Carlisle, the Washington attorney who advised the regents on such matters.[1]

Cameron, a New Yorker, had been brought down to Washington by Renwick after they had worked together in New York on the

*Figure 29. Captain Barton S. Alexander,
United States Army Corps of Engineers.*

architect's Calvary Church, but the contractor did not wish to return north. Cameron, like Renwick, had used his time in Washington well. He served as superintendent on Renwick's Trinity Episcopal Church, begun in 1850, and as contractor for the United States Soldiers' Home—an Italianate design by Lieutenant Barton S. Alexander—in 1851. Cameron had other investments of his own as well. Buying land just south of the Smithsonian site, at B and Tenth Streets, S.W., he built two row houses in the Greek Revival style. Cameron lived in one and rented the other, and apparently found his life in Washington to be so comfortable that he did not want it disturbed.[2]

At length, Carlisle reported back to the Board of Regents, advising that Cameron was within his rights to complete the contract. Unsettled by this news, they turned for a second opinion to the United States District Attorney, P. R. Fendall, who agreed with Carlisle. Renwick's interpretation of the contract as "complete" was thus held to be invalid, and the regents were stuck with the contractor.[3]

Joseph Henry consoled himself with the fact that Cameron "had previously given an estimate of the amount for which he could do the work, which was considerably lower than that of the Architect." Such a promise led Henry to consider it "safest and best under all the circumstances of the case, to allow him to go on," especially since Captain Alexander would be "daily on the ground to ensure a faithful performance of the contract." Henry still would not trust Cameron alone with the building, but the contractor did have "all the materials at hand, and being well acquainted with all parts of the structure as it now stands, [would be] enabled to do the work at a lower rate than any other person." But when the question later came up of converting the east wing of the building into a residence for the Secretary, the regents made quite clear their intention to entrust the work to another contractor.[4]

The delay caused by Cameron's desire to continue with the Castle gave the regents a great deal of time to decide what to do with their main building. There was a consensus that a new lecture room should be built, though its placement would be problematic. In accordance with the original agreement that brought Henry to Washington, General Totten proposed in March 1853 that the east wing be renovated to house the Secretary and his family. And in an effort to make the main building fireproof, it was agreed that the entire frame of woodwork should be removed from the interior of the building.

In early June, 1853, Henry and Bache traveled to Philadelphia with Captain Montgomery C. Meigs to study the acoustics of public buildings in that city. Meigs had been appointed as Superintendent of the Capitol Extension by Secretary of War Jefferson Davis in late March, and the trip to Philadelphia was primarily concerned with the acoustics of the new House and Senate chambers. But the journey would allow for speculations about new lecture rooms as well.[5]

When Henry returned to Washington on June 17, 1853, work had been once again under way for four days. Henry arrived after dark and, exhausted, gave no attention to the building that night. Morning's light, however, revealed "great changes in the appearance of the Institution Building. . . . Two large openings have been made in the south side into which carts are driven for the purpose of excavating the basement. All the timber of the interior of the main building will be removed by the end of next week." By the middle of July, Henry could write to Bache that the "forest of timber which filled the interior" had been "entirely removed," and that the roof had been braced up. "The earth has also been dug away from the floor to the depth of several feet in order to form a basement. The whole is now one vast concavity, two hundred feet long, fifty feet wide, and seventy feet high." He also reported that strong winds and frequent changes in pressure had "broken a number of the sashes of the flimsy Renwickian windows."[6]

With the interior completely removed once again, the time had come for a decision on the placement of the new lecture room. Considerations of crowd control had led to a preference that the hall be placed on the first floor, and in 1851 the building committee had ordered that the large doors of the main entrance "be made to open outwards, in order to avoid the fatal consequences sometimes occasioned by the rushing out in panic of a large crowd of individuals." But the very size of the room was an obstacle, since it could "not be fitted up without two rows of pillars of considerable dimensions, which would materially intercept the view, and affect the character of the room as regards sound. Various plans have been proposed for getting rid of these pillars, but we think there would be a want of perfect security in adopting them." The building committee finally

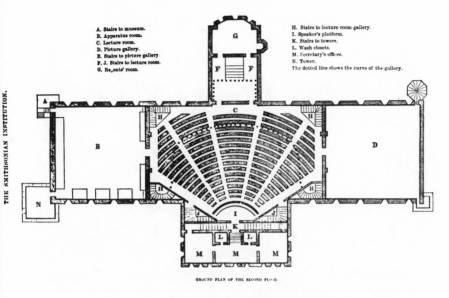

A. Stairs to museum.
B. Apparatus room.
C. Lecture room.
D. Picture gallery.
E. Stairs to picture gallery.
F, J. Stairs to lecture room.
G. Regents' room.

H. Stairs to lecture room gallery.
I. Speaker's platform.
K. Stairs to towers.
L. Wash closets.
M. Secretary's offices.
N. Tower.
The dotted line shows the curve of the gallery.

GROUND PLAN OF THE SECOND FLOOR

Figure 30. Barton S. Alexander-Joseph Henry, Smithsonian Building. Ground plan of the second floor. 1853.

decided to build one large lecture room on the second floor, flanked by the art gallery on the west and a chemical apparatus room on the east (fig. 30). The museum was to have the undivided use of the first floor, to be called the Great Hall.[7]

Having learned from nearly six years of building that the relative growth of the library and museum were unpredictable, and half hoping that the government would purchase the building for use as a museum, the building committee observed that "should the building ever be required for other purposes, such as an entire museum or library, the division walls could easily be removed, and the whole space converted into one large room." The first floor, although designated for the exclusive use of the museum, could be divided "into two apartments, with a central hall or wide passage in between," in case the library overflowed the west wing and range.

Spencer Baird, diligently mounting his animals, was not pleased with the new arrangements. To George Perkins Marsh he wrote in November 1853, "I much regret that the upper story of the build-

Figure 31. Barton S. Alexander-Joseph Henry, Smithsonian Building. The Lecture Room. 1854–1855.

ing is to be converted into a great lecture room [fig. 31] with a few adjacent offices, and a portion only of the corner allotted to the museum." He cast covetous eyes on the east wing, but observed that "Professor Henry wishes to convert that into a dwelling house for himself."[8]

Baird was also well aware that a movement was afoot for the government to buy the entire building. The commissioner of patents had approached Henry in October 1853 informing him that the "rooms now occupied by the museum of the exploring expedition was required for other purposes, and that the government might better purchase the buildings of the Institution than to put up another edifice." Henry was rather dubious that such a bill could pass the Congress, but admitted to Bache that it "would be a very desirable arrangement for the Institution to get rid of the museum and library and have twelve or fifteen thousand dollars added to its income." The commissioner of patents, perhaps sensing the political impossibility of persuading Congress to buy the building, proposed instead a $15,000 appropriation for the Smithsonian to take care of the collections of the Patent Office. Still others, Baird informed Marsh, were "in favor of creating a grand crystal palace between the Smithsonian and [the Washington] monument." As for Baird, he would accept a crystal palace, a Norman castle, anything he could get: "I don't much care how they manage it, [as long as] *I* can have charge of the Natural History Collections."[9]

While the extramural dickering continued, rapid progress was being made on the interior of the building. A brick sewer was run through the middle of the building, and by the end of 1853 all the masonry and most of the brickwork was completed. Concerning Captain Alexander's efforts at fireproofing, the building committee concluded that he had "successfully evinced in this work a combination of practical skill and scientific knowledge." And on the whole, the committee found that the work had "been prosecuted with great vigor." Still to be completed were the stairways to the lecture room and its gallery (see in fig. 30: F, H, and J), additional support for the roof, flooring, plastering, and painting, and seats for the lecture room. Captain Alexander opined that "should nothing happen to prevent it, the building will be finished during the present year [1854], and at a cost within the estimate."[10]

In January 1854, the difficulties with the contractor, Gilbert Cameron, were finally resolved. At their annual meeting, the regents were informed by a letter from J. M. Carlisle that the suit between Cameron and John Sniffin, in which the regents had been named as a party, had been dismissed. The judge had ruled, Carlisle noted, that the Board of Regents could not be sued. Cameron promptly applied for the payments that had been withheld from him pending the outcome of the suit. The subject was referred to a committee, which decided in March to pay the balance, and Henry did so after a detailed examination of the account.[11]

Even as one problem was dispatched, another of much greater magnitude loomed up. In March 1853, the regents had created a special committee which was to examine the distribution of income of the Institution and report of "such changes, if any, as in their opinion are desirable." The make-up of the committee made unlikely a recommendation of increased expenditures for the library or the museum. Henry saw the matter as a test of his authority and his plans for the Institution. He claimed to regret "more and more that

I was obliged to give way, in accordance with the law of Congress, to the establishment of a museum and library, and I am determined while I have any direction in the operations that they shall be entirely subordinate to the publications and other active operations." [12]

By no means opposed to museums and libraries in general, Henry objected to such activities' being forced onto the Smithsonian against his will. He hoped to "see in due time a general museum in this city supported by the government, which will relieve this Institution from the charge of Collections." Toward that end Henry developed a plan to enlarge the museum in the Patent Office "in order to obviate the necessity of expending the Smithsonian income on objects of this kind." As for Choate's great library, Henry looked to the Library of Congress as an expanding collection under the care of the federal government. Nevertheless, Choate and Jewett were not likely to give up their budding library at the Smithsonian without a fight. [13]

Even before the special committee reported, everyone involved knew what was coming (see fig. 32). Spencer Baird wrote in February 1854, "How they can report in favor of removing the restrictions in favor of the Library [and] Museum with the plain law before them I cannot see. Perhaps their vision is sharper than mine." The old book man, Rufus Choate, who had not attended a meeting of the Board of Regents for several years, unsheathed his pen to protest to the attorney general "against the abandonment of the plan, according to which, there is to be surely, slowly, under an unalterable law, accumulation at Washington, the noblest collection of Books, Manuscripts and specimens of Art in the world. This is to build our Capital of Marble that shall not fall." Privately Choate wrote to Jewett that he could not "comprehend the reasons on which the compromise is sought to be disturbed." Jewett himself saw the recent development in cataclysmic terms, claiming that "Professor Henry is pushing his plans in such a way as to put in imminent peril the very existence of the Institution. How it will all end it is impossible to see, but the whole matter is to me ineffably disgusting and I would rather dig clams for a living than stay here as of late." [14]

In early March 1854, Jewett and Baird received a request from the select committee for a statement on the issues under considera-

Figure 32. James Renwick, Jr., Smithsonian Building. The Library. ca. 1855.

tion. Baird wrote out a brief statement, but that of Jewett (fig. 33) ran to fifty pages. When it was delivered to the committee on the eve of its meeting, Senator James A. Pearce informed the other committee members that Jewett's communication was "of so extraordinary a character as to require a reference to Professor Henry for an answer, and accordingly postponed the meeting until this should be received." [15]

Henry, for his part, dismissed Jewett's statements as "filled with quibbles, false statements and abuse of myself and my plans. It will

Figure 33. Charles Coffin Jewett, Assistant Secretary for the Library.

do him harm and induce me to set before the Regents more fully than I have done the selfish and unwarranted assumptions of those who were appointed by myself as assistants." In the eyes of the Secretary, the principal virtue of Baird's report was its brevity, and he had no doubt that "when I have settled with Jewett," Baird could be brought "to a sense of his duty." Even in the heat of battle, Henry maintained that he had no wish to abandon the museum "unless we can induce Congress to establish one on a better scale." He reiterated, however, that the museum must be "subordinate to the active operations. The same with the Library. But I am determined that my assistants shall know their places."[16]

Six weeks elapsed without a meeting. Finally, on April 29, 1854, as debate raged in the Congress over the Kansas-Nebraska bill, Regents James Meacham, William H. English, and David Stuart, who were anxious to preserve the compromise with the book men, were able to force a meeting. The Executive Committee recommended an

uneven distribution of appropriations "because the compromise resolutions which require such equality of distribution do not go into
effect until the completion of the building." The special committee
on the distribution of income requested more time for study. Senator Pearce presented the report on May twentieth. A great library,
the committee concluded, "would be the *hiving* of knowledge, not
its increase and diffusion. . . . It would not of itself add to the sum
of human knowledge, it would not increase the stores of learning,
but only bring them together. It would develop no new truths,
reveal no hidden laws of nature, but only contain the record of what
might already be known; so that in no proper sense could it be said
to increase knowledge." The committee thus soundly endorsed the
views of Joseph Henry and called for their thorough application.
Although it seemed clear that a majority of regents favored the report, Rufus Choate succeeded in delaying a vote on the accompany-
ing resolutions until July 8, which might have conceivably left time
to work out a compromise.[17]

Jewett did not give up hope, even though the inevitable result of
the next meeting would be the abandonment of the compromise.
On June 15 he wrote to George Livermore, excusing his "hasty
note" with a reminder that he was "very hard at work preparing for
the 8th of July." When the regents gathered in the early-morning
July heat, they were presented almost immediately with a resolution
declaring that "whilst power is reserved in the said section" of the
original legislation "to the Board of Regents, to remove both the
Secretary and his assistants, in the opinion of the Board, power,
nevertheless, remains with the Secretary to remove his said assistants." Congressman English suggested that the resolution be amended
by adding the words "with the consent of the Board of Regents,"
after the words, "power, nevertheless, remains with the Secretary."
The amendment failed to pass, and the book men attempted to
delay the vote on the resolution. This too failed, and the regents
affirmed, on a six to four vote, the authority of the Secretary to
remove his subordinates. Two days later, Henry wrote Jewett his
letter of dismissal.[18]

Not one to surrender easily, Jewett wrote to each individual regent on July 31, 1854, denying that the Board had the authority
to delegate such power to the Secretary, and Jewett, acting on his
own authority, declared it a "mere nullity." He informed the regents

that "as soon as the restoration of my health shall permit, I shall be ready to resume my duties as 'Assistant Secretary to act as librarian of the Smithsonian Institution'; and that I shall continue to claim the salary fixed as compensation for my services in that office." [19]

Nor was Jewett the only fired subordinate complaining to the board. Lorin Blodget had been hired to assist in the collection of meteorological observations. Henry had paid him as a temporary employee of the Institution, but upon the termination of his services, Blodget insisted that the calculations which he had performed with Smithsonian data were his own property, for which he expected remuneration and recognition. Blodget and Jewett both hoped to take their case to the Congress when it returned in January. Henry wrote to Bache in November that they were "confident of success and one of their friends was surprised to be told by Mr. Peale that he did not think Mr. Jewett had any chance of being reinstated in his former position." [20]

The building by November 1854 was very close to completion, a fact that filled Joseph Henry with relief. "It will be a great comfort to be rid of contractors and the dirt and rubbish of building materials." Despite a "cost considerably more than the estimate of the architect," Henry thought that the lecture room was "by far the best in this country. It ought to satisfy the city." As for the architect, Captain Alexander, Henry considered him to have been "very successful in conducting the work. The only objection I have to his professional character is that he is rather too extravagant, having been used to the purse of the government." His meditation on the expense of the building led Henry into a revery about the "depravity of the human heart." He observed a "remarkable state of loose morality relative to all transactions with the government or with establishments connected with it. The property of the government is everybody's property and every one considers himself entitled to a share." [21]

In his year-end report Captain Alexander emphasized the "great simplicity" of the rooms of the central building. "There is not much ornament, but still enough, I think, to enable the building to do its duty with grace and dignity." Alexander also reminded the regents that the "lower hall is equally adapted to the purposes of a museum or a library." Unless the Congress reversed the decision to fire Jewett, that space, the Great Hall, would go to Baird and the museum.[22]

With the great lecture room on the second floor of the main building completed, the regents moved on the plans to convert the east wing into a residence for the Secretary. They hired William Chopin in 1855 to carry out the changes, on a separate contract from that of Cameron. The entire wing was split into two stories, with the Secretary and his family housed on the upper story, and the lower story used to receive and distribute all the articles of exchange, and to hold extra copies of Institution publications.[23]

When the regents assembled for their annual meeting in January 1855, they did so for the first time in the Regents' Room in the south tower of the central building, the only room left intact from David Dale Owen's plan. They took up the resolutions that had been offered the year before by the special committee on the division of income. These resolutions had been tabled after the climactic vote on the resolution giving the Secretary the authority to fire his subordinates. Both Rufus Choate and James Meacham attended, putting the book men at their full strength of six, but it was not enough to prevent the repeal of the requirement of an equal division of income between Henry's "active" operations and the museum and library. The next day, Senator Pearce of the Executive Committee reported on the case of Lorin Blodget, concluding that Henry had been well within his rights in dealing with Blodget. Henry himself informed the regents that he "had deemed it his duty since the last session to remove Mr. Jewett from the office of assistant to the Secretary." Senator Pearce immediately offered a resolution regretting the "necessity of Mr. Jewett's removal," and also approving it. The regents adjourned without acting on the proposal, but the outcome was not in doubt. Rufus Choate went home to write his letter of resignation from the Board of Regents.[24]

Two weeks later the regents received word from the Congress that a select committee had been named to investigate "whether the Smithsonian Institution has been managed, and its funds expended, in accordance with the law establishing the institution." Charles W. Upham, a congressman from Massachusetts sympathetic to the views of Choate, was appointed chairman of the committee. They held hearings each evening through February, with Meacham, Jewett, and Blodget leading the attack and Secretary Henry and Senators Pearce and Mason on the defense of the Institution. Rufus Choate, back in Massachusetts, was too ill to attend, and could only write to Upham, entreating him "to do two things. 1. vindicate the sense of the law. 2. vindicate art, taste, learning, genius, mind, history, ethnology, morals—against Sciolists, chemists, & catchers of extinct skunks." Jewett and Blodget demanded that Henry produce all papers relative to the case, until Senator Pearce observed that the table was groaning under the burden of the paper.[25]

The committee even called the Institution architect, Captain Alexander, to testify. Representative Meacham cross-examined Alexander concerning the amount of room set aside for the library in various plans. Alexander reminded him that the large room on the first floor of the main building was "equally adapted to a library or a museum." With the end of the session bearing down on them, testimony was cut short, and the three congressmen who had heard the testimony agreed to write two reports. Congressman Upham was the sole signer of the "majority" report, which pled for the reinstatement of the compromise. Turned in to the House on the last day of the session, the report was immediately lost in the shuffle, and Jewett's cause was lost with it. The ex-librarian wrote to Charles Folsom of the Boston Athenaeum that the "malice & meanness of my enemies have prevailed to defeat & destroy this great literary project upon which I had bestowed so much time, toil & money— just at the moment when a few weeks longer continuance of my authority in regard to it would have placed it beyond their power. It makes me sick to think of it."[26]

For Joseph Henry, it was another hard-won victory. Much vilification was indulged in by both sides, but in the end it simplified Henry's world: he was no longer forced to contend with Jewett or with his prime supporters on the Board of Regents, Rufus Choate and James Meacham. The latter never tendered his resignation, as had Choate, but Meacham did not attend a meeting of the Board of Regents after January 1855, and was not reappointed by the Speaker of the House in 1856.

Spencer Baird had refused to join Jewett and Blodget in their accusations, and testified only unwillingly. His working relationship with Henry was thus preserved, although the Secretary's attitude toward the library and museum remained unchanged: the government, he insisted, should support a large library and a great museum, but separate from the Smithsonian. As long as Washington went without a suitable government repository for the collections held at the Patent Office, the Smithsonian would be in dire danger of becoming a museum, but for now Henry had once again prevailed. He had reshaped the east wing and the main building to suit his plan for the Institution. He had regained authority over the west wing and its library through his clash with Jewett. Having moved into full control of the Institution, Henry moved his family into the east wing of the Castle, his home for the rest of his life.

Chapter Eight

✖

NOT BY ITS
CASTELLATED BUILDING

WITH the demise of the book men, Joseph Henry finally had
the full support of the Board of Regents, and full authority
over the assistant secretary, Spencer F. Baird. He was still unable,
however, to control the forces outside of the Institution which mil-
itated in favor of declaring the Smithsonian to be the National Museum. Eventually Henry succeeded in loaning the library and the
art gallery, more or less permanently, to the Library of Congress and
to the nascent Corcoran Gallery of Art. But as quickly as Henry
could dispose of such collections, Spencer Baird filled the vacant
space with museum exhibits. The Secretary segregated his "active"
operations in the east wing, and left the main building and the west
wing to Baird; by this internal arrangement he hoped to demon-
strate that the real Smithsonian Institution, the clearinghouse of
scientific research, had no need for such a large building. When
Baird had filled the building to its rafters, he and Henry lobbied
for a second building, either adjacent or attached to the Castle, so
that any National Museum would necessarily require the use of both.
To the very end, Joseph Henry desired the government to buy the
building or somehow free his Institution from its architectural burden.

Joseph Henry found his apartments in the Smithsonian Building
to be "very pleasant and commodious," or at least he claimed as
much in urging Asa Gray and his wife to come visit. In the summer
of 1856, however, a "very disagreeable odor" permeated the east

wing of the building, including the Secretary's living quarters. The source of the offensive smell was the main sewer, and it was noticed that the intensity of the odor depended on the tides of the Potomac. The high tide forced the sewer gasses back into the building, where they seeped through the "crevices of the encasing brick-work." Consequently a vent was placed along the sewer line, allowing the gasses another outlet.[1]

When not coping with unpleasant smells, the Secretary turned his attention to the question of a National Museum. In his *Report* for 1856, Henry observed that the best course of action would be for the federal government to buy the Castle to house the collections in the Patent Office, or even for the Smithsonian to give the building away if "for no other consideration than that of being relieved from the costly charge of the collections." Nevertheless, Henry offered to display the museum of the Wilkes expedition in the Great Hall—which occupied the entire first floor of the main building— if the "appropriation now annually made for the preservation and display of the collections" were to be continued under the direction of the regents. Henry's earlier plan to make the museum of the Wilkes expedition so impressive that it would become the nucleus of a separate National Museum had fallen through, but even though Henry now welcomed the collections of the Patent Office under his own roof, he still hoped to avoid the expenditure of Smithsonian funds on the museum. When in 1857 Congress appropriated $17,000 for museum cases and for the transfer and arrangement of the collections, Henry wrote to Asa Gray that "if we can make the establishment popular I doubt not that in due time we shall be relieved from the expense, if not the care, of the museum."[2]

The cases were installed, for the most part, by the end of 1857, though the transfer of collections did not begin until the summer of 1858. The building committee claimed that the cases formed a "beautiful addition to the large hall, and are apparently well adapted to the purpose for which they are intended" (fig. 34). Also expanding in the Castle were the accommodations for the library. The west wing was "furnished with alcoves and a gallery extending around three sides of the large room. This arrangement, which will serve very much to increase the accommodation and security of the books, produces a very pleasing architectural effect."[3]

Figure 34. Smithsonian Building. The Great Hall, with museum exhibits. ca. 1872.

The building committee was not so kind in its discussion of the "peculiar style of architecture of the building." Owing to "the large amount of surface it exposes to the weather," they claimed, "constant repairs" were necessary. "During the past year almost the whole time of two workmen has been occupied in this service." The picturesque turrets and towers may have been expressive of internal function, but they also made work in a way not anticipated by the Owen brothers.

As the cases of the Great Hall began to fill, Henry was negotiating on yet another item for display: the Indian paintings of John Mix Stanley. Although he had spent ten years in the southwest, painting portraits of members of forty-three Indian tribes, Stanley was deeply in debt and on the verge of selling off his collection to appease his creditors. Henry advanced $1200 on the paintings, hoping "that the Regents would assume the debt . . . until such time as the government should be interested in purchasing them"; when the regents thought this inadvisable, Henry personally assigned the debt. The Secretary was interested in the paintings for their anthropological value, and placed them in the art gallery on the west end of the second floor amidst cases containing "specimens of Indian costume, implements of war, and other articles to illustrate Indian manners and customs." Noting that the paintings formed an "object of attraction and interest to the numerous visitors of the Institution," Henry hoped that the government would one day find the means to purchase the collection.[4]

On the question of an art gallery, as on those of a library and museum, Henry was an advocate of government support and an opponent of Smithsonian support. In early 1861, as Washington awaited the arrival of President-elect Abraham Lincoln, Henry took note of the "large and elegant building," rising near the White House, destined to be the Corcoran Gallery of Art. He proposed to "lend the influence of the Institution in procuring specimens of art for [Corcoran's] gallery," a suggestion that would not seem to imply the lending of paintings; however, when Joseph Henry came to refer to *any* building by James Renwick, Jr., as "large and elegant," the Secretary must have had ulterior motives. He revealed his hand in the next year's *Annual Report*, where he wrote that "it would be proper . . . to deposit in [Corcoran's] collection the specimens which might belong to this establishment." Unfortunately for Henry, his scheme was upset by the outbreak of the Civil War. William Wilson Corcoran, a Southern sympathizer—and, like Henry and Bache, a good friend of Jefferson Davis and other Confederates—decided to spend the war years in Europe. The federal government then seized several Washington buildings owned by Corcoran, including his then-unfinished private Gallery of Art, which was initially used as a depot for military stores.[5]

As the staff and the reputation of the Smithsonian Institution continued to grow, a number of small rooms in the three largest towers of the main building were used as sleeping quarters for men who either worked at the Smithsonian or had temporary business there. The longest stay was that of Fielding B. Meek, a paleontologist who worked on the collections of various expeditions and who in return asked only for space at a work table and an apartment for sleeping. He lived in the Castle from 1858 until his death in 1876. The Secretary approved of the policy up to a point, but by 1863 he could write Baird that the "making [of] the Smithsonian building a caravansarai has been carried a little too far."[6]

The appeal of living in a sandstone castle apparently escaped Henry, for his own accommodations tended to grow intolerably hot in the summer. The walls of the building, with their extremely long southern exposure, "continue to grow hotter and hotter from the beginning to the end of the hot term until they become like the sides of an oven—in a condition to cook whatever they contain." Indeed, Henry wrote to Bache that the temperature in his bedroom at midnight was ninety-one on at least one occasion.[7]

Atmospheric extremes were common in the castle, because the building's heating system was not sufficient for Washington winters. The twenty-fourth of January, 1865, was an all-too-typical winter day, bitterly cold. Workmen installing new cases in the art gallery at the west end of the second story of the main building carried a stove from the apparatus room at the opposite end of the floor. Secretary Henry spent the morning close by his own stove, dictating his *Annual Report* to the chief clerk, William J. Rhees.

Shortly after two, a lady from Detroit called on the Secretary wishing to see the Stanley Indian portraits and to confer with Henry "as to the propriety of selling them to the Legislature of Michigan." Ever encouraging government promotion of the arts, Henry accompanied her to the gallery (fig. 35) where the workmen had just completed their task. The new cases lined the wall and formed a platform, accessible by ladder, above which the paintings were hung. The Secretary and his guest were soon joined by Rhees, who wished to see the new arrangement of the pictures. "After some conversa-

Figure 35. Smithsonian Building. The Gallery of Art.

tion with the professor as to the appearance of the room," Rhees returned to the office to warm himself by the stove.[8]

Henry came back to his office a little before three, in time to greet another visitor. A "loud crackling noise" over their heads startled the group, and Rhees thought momentarily that it was the "sliding of ice upon the roof," but Henry thought it sounded like fire. The visitor had noticed a burning smell as he climbed the stairs. The noise increased and the three rushed to the door leading to the lecture room. The hall, Rhees remembered, "was quite dark." The Secretary exclaimed, "The house is on fire. Sound the fire alarm." With that he ran down the stairs toward the telegraph alarm. Rhees headed back to the Secretary's office in the north tower, retrieved a box containing some bonds deposited there for safekeeping, and took them downstairs.

In the basement, machinist William De Buest, carpenter T. N. Woltz, and laborer Roger Sullivan were repairing a sled when De Buest noticed smoke passing by the door. He ran outside, followed by the others, but could see nothing until he was beyond the south tower. Dense smoke rose from the western end of the roof of the main building. Running to the picture gallery, De Buest saw no fire, but the skylight in the lecture room was clouded, and he could hear the roar of the flame. He returned to the basement, got out the telegraph key and sent the alarm. After giving the key to his son Robert with instructions to repeat the message, De Buest and the others returned to the gallery. The ladder used to hang the pictures above the cases rested against the south wall, and De Buest climbed it and began handing down paintings to the watchman, Henry Horan, and to Sullivan and Woltz. As the trio began the trek from the gallery, a 6-foot square of ceiling fell into the room exposing the blazing rafters. The three chose not to make a second trip.

Spencer Baird had entered the basement just as the workmen discovered the fire, and hastened to the offices in the east wing to rouse Fielding Meek and Henry Elliott. Meek rushed upstairs, and helped a group force open a door that led to the gallery of the lecture room, then went downstairs to fetch two of the twenty-four buckets of water the Secretary had placed around the building. Not until he had started back with them did Meek notice that the water in the buckets was frozen solid. He left the buckets and returned to the lecture room, but it was quickly becoming apparent that the fire would not be extinguished by a few pails of water, solid or liquid. Meek and the others turned to saving whatever documents and apparatus they could.

Baird returned to his office in the east wing to bundle up the museum catalogues, unpublished manuscripts, and correspondence, and sent them out with volunteers who happened by. Out went the japanned boxes containing some sixty bird skins, and a case of Saint Lucas birds. When Baird came back for a second load he found that the bookcases in his office and the adjoining workroom had been broken into and the contents dropped out of the window into the cloister on the north side of the range, where another group tossed them onto the lawn, With the aid of a policeman, Baird put a halt to the book brigade.

Others on the staff scrambled to save what they could from their sleeping apartments. Fielding Meek carried down a trunk from his room in the south tower to the east wing, then headed back for his bedding. As he passed the lecture room, the plastering fell from the ceiling, making the flames plainly visible.

By this time, the firemen, police, and a large number of military men had arrived on the scene, and Joseph Henry began giving orders. The Secretary had feared for the library, which had already been locked by an assistant, Theodore N. Gill, but the winds drove the flames eastward, toward Henry's residence. He "hastened to learn the condition of my family. Our house was for some time in great danger. The furniture was removed. Fortunately a group of cavalry and a detachment of soldiers were ordered on the ground for the protection of this property." Alas, not everyone was so concerned about the protection of property. The private room of William Stimpson, who was in Chicago at the time of the fire, was broken into so that access could be gained to the roof over the apparatus room. Later, firemen or volunteers rummaged through Stimpson's belongings, and consumed some whiskey used for preserving specimens. As the Secretary observed, they were "repaid for the use of this by the effect of the sulphate of copper which had been dissolved in it. Several of them became deadly sick and would have died had they not vomited."[9]

At length, the fire was brought under control. The crowds still milled around long after sundown, while furniture, books, and apparatus were carried back inside. The Secretary and his wife Harriet remained up all night. Having caught a cold in the afternoon, Henry also had severe cramps and was confined to his bed for most of the following morning.[10]

The fire caused the collapse of the roof as well as gutting of the second floor of the main building. But the ranges and the wings were spared, and the specimens in the museum on the first floor, though damp from leakage of water from the second story, were in good condition. The only thing that had prevented the entire building from burning down was the fireproof masonry-encased iron beams that Barton S. Alexander had installed in 1853 and 1854. Had not the floor fallen down in 1850, the whole of the interior would have been consumed in 1865. The masonry and iron beams supporting the second floor held when the roof came crashing onto it; they also withstood the test of fire.

Secretary Henry estimated that at least forty or fifty thousand copies of letters he had written or received were lost in the fire, along "with a large number of reports of all my experiments upon oils." Dr. Hare's chemical apparatuses were lost, as were the libraries of Beaufort, South Carolina, and of Bishop Johns from Fairfax Theological Seminary, which had been seized during the Civil War and deposited at the Smithsonian by the Secretary of War for safekeeping.[11]

Perhaps the worst blow was the almost total loss of the art gallery. Of John Mix Stanley's two hundred portraits of Indians, then worth $20,000, a mere seven were saved. Charles Bird King's paintings of prominent Indians who had visited Washington, works executed at the expense of the Indian Bureau, were all lost. King had died three years before the fire, but Stanley had to bear not only the emotional brunt of his losses, but the financial brunt as well. The government had never acted upon his offer to sell the pictures, and he had been "on the point of obtaining a grant from the Legislature of Michigan for its purchase" when the disaster struck. Henry wrote to the artist in March about the "sad catastrophe, which destroyed, in a few moments, the result of many years of your labours. I need not say that I am profoundly grieved on account of your irreparable loss, as well as my own, in the destruction of my papers."

With the main building roofless, Henry could not stay bedridden for long. On the evening after the fire he was making the rounds, calling on political allies, particularly the chancellor of the Smithsonian, Chief Justice Salmon P. Chase, and Secretary of the Treasury William P. Fessenden. Next he paid a visit to Secretary of War Edwin M. Stanton, requesting the assistance of the army in raising a temporary roof. Stanton replied that he "would not do this without the consent of the President and he would not direct the work to be done unless it was paid for."[12]

Waiting for Henry on his return to the Castle was a letter from Colonel Barton S. Alexander. Since seeing Henry that morning, Alexander had been engaged in ascertaining the cause of the fire, which he found to be manifest: the smoke pipe in the stove temporarily placed in the art gallery had been connected not into a flue but into the brick lining—and this had sent smoke and sparks billowing up into the rafters of the attic, allowing the fire to spread unnoticed.[13]

Alexander urged that certain measures be taken immediately "to prevent further damage, particularly to the museum." He proposed to remove the debris in the upper arches supporting the second floor, take down the two brick walls which enclosed the lecture room, remove any brick or stone in any danger of falling, and throw up a temporary roof. "Unless this is done," he warned, "the water from snow and rain will penetrate the arches, and perhaps ruin them, or at least loosen the plastering on the ceiling below and cause it to fall with serious damage." Alexander estimated that thirty or forty men could "clear away the debris in a couple of days. And then with the addition of a like number of carpenters the roof can be put on in two more days." Alexander concluded his consultation with Henry with a discussion of the appropriate channels in the Department of War through which the needed work would be authorized, but Henry, having mulled over his unproductive meeting with Secretary Stanton, planned a more direct approach.

The next day the Secretary went to the White House for a conference with President Lincoln. Not only did the president express "much sympathy on account of the accident," but he also had words with the Secretary of War. Before the day was out, Alexander received a directive from Stanton ordering him to render any assistance to the Smithsonian "not incompatible with his duty to the service." Stanton also informed Quartermaster General Montgomery C. Meigs of the president's wishes; Meigs relayed them to Assistant Quartermaster General Daniel H. Rucker; Rucker immediately corralled Edward Clark, who had supervised Thomas U. Walter's west wing and his own north wing of the Patent Office, to supervise the raising of the temporary roof over the Castle. General Rucker also "detailed a large force of carpenters and laborers," and, true to Alexander's estimate, the task was completed by the last day of January. The cleanup and construction of the temporary roof cost the Institution just over $3000. Fielding B. Meek wrote that with the temporary roof on and with the walls and towers still standing, apparently uninjured, "from a hasty glance, looking over from the City, you might not notice anything wrong" (see fig. 36).

By the end of the month, the Secretary was beginning to see ways in which the fire could work to his advantage. To Louis Agassiz he wrote that the "accident, though much to be lamented, will I think in the end be of advantage to the Institution. So long as the building was covered with a wooden roof and the wings liable to destruction from fire the property contained in it was not safe." Henry now anticipated putting on a metal roof, and entirely rearranging the upper story, "placing within the fire proof portion of the building

Figure 36. Smithsonian Building, roofless, January 25–31, 1865.

all articles of value and cutting these off from the wings by means
of iron doors." The Secretary even speculated that the roof would
have eventually caught fire anyway, "at some future time, when the
contents of the rooms below would have been of much greater value." [14]

Through February and into March the Secretary was "very busily
engaged in consulting architects and builders" as he sought to go
beyond restoration by improving upon the original building. At
length the building committee chose Adolph Cluss as the architect
for the project. Cluss was a German émigré, and his Washington
practice had included design and supervision of the principal schools
and markets of the city during the Civil War years and afterwards. [15]

The building committee began a survey of the walls, which "forced
upon the committee the conviction that the original construction of
the building, as a whole, was very defective, and, in many respects,
unsuited as a receptacle of records and other valuable articles, the

loss of which could never be repaired." Not only was the second story of the main building destroyed, but in addition the roofs and interiors of the two central north towers and the south tower had collapsed during the fire. The building committee also discovered that the cornice atop the south tower was merely sitting there, and had never been attached to anything; part of it had fallen down. Worse, the survey revealed a "vertical crack extending a considerable portion of the height" of the tallest north tower, the Flag Tower (fig. 20). The walls of the entire main building were lined with brickwork, not fastened to either the interior or exterior walls, and the building committee decided to pack the 9-inch space in the two central north towers with brickwork and cement. The top 30 feet of the south tower had to be pulled down, and Cluss set to work completely rebuilding the north wall of the south tower.[16]

The three principal large towers were a higher priority than the second story because they served as office space for the Secretary and his staff. Moreover, Henry did not wish to rebuild the lecture room at all. In 1862 he had written that the "existence of the Lecture Room in the Smithsonian building has been during the last two years a source of much trouble and I hope at the next meeting of the Regents some definite rules will be adopted for my guidance in the intervals between sessions of the Board." The problem, he told Congressman William English, was that it was "impossible to keep a large room of that kind from being used for other than scientific purposes. The citizens of Washington ought to provide for themselves a room for public meetings." Henry's intention was to let the second story remain a shell until Congress could be "induced to appropriate [it] either to the museum of the Medical Department or that of the Agricultural Bureau."[17]

By mid-July 1865, the workmen were ready to begin restoration of the towers. Difficulties in procuring iron beams for supports had delayed the start, but Henry hoped that the office space provided by the towers would once again be in use by the end of the year. "The temporary roof," on the other hand, would "serve to protect the main building until next summer, and if we confine the repairs for the present to the parts above mentioned, we shall have funds sufficient to carry us through the year without selling any of our stock." The repairs were expected to cost at least $125,000, but the figure began to climb when the architect, Adolph Cluss, informed

Henry that the "floor of the west wing, on which the copyright books are placed, is about to give way." The Secretary concluded it necessary to replace the floor with one of brick and iron, and observed to Rhees that "had the fire not occurred we should have had to replace the floors" of the north and south towers of the main building, because the "beams could not have much longer supported the flagging."[18]

In the summer of 1866, bids were taken for the iron roof and tower supports. The lowest offer was from the Phoenix Iron Company of Philadelphia, and a contract was signed in July. Because of "unexpected delays the iron frame was not received until too late in the season for putting on the slate, without injury to the cement by frost." The end of the building season found none of the burned out rooms back in use, but by April 1867 Henry could predict, accurately, that the "whole will be completed, with the exception of the large room on the second story, by the end of the present year. We are pressing the workmen to finish the towers in which are the rooms wanted for the operations of the Institution."[19]

The building was rebuilt by the end of 1867, and the chairman of the building committee, General Richard Delafield, declared the "plans, material and workmanship are of a satisfactory character, alike creditable to the talents and careful supervision of Mr. Cluss, the architect." In the course of the repairs, however, Cluss had discovered that the battlements which lined the roof of the Castle had not been equipped with gutters, and, in the absence of proper drainage, leaks through the roof were common. The funds of the Institution would not permit Cluss to attack this problem, but the building committee warned that "until it is done . . . the building is not secure, nor the property within it, from dampness and moisture."[20]

The repair work on the building actually increased the amount of work space. The north tower, formerly two stories, was divided into seven. The south tower still contained the Regents' Room, and the first floor became an extension of the Great Hall for the museum. Ceilings were dropped in the south tower to create six stories instead of the previous four. As a result the new rooms were lighted by an old method: circular holes were cut in the walls to form "bull's eye" windows, "without interfering with the original architectural effect of the exterior."[21]

The fire served to emphasize to the Board of Regents that the Smithsonian library was less than secure in the west wing, which was not fireproof. At the next year's meeting of the regents, in February 1866, Congressman James W. Patterson recommended that the library be secured "from danger of destruction" by placing it, "under proper restrictions, in the Library of Congress." A committee was appointed, with Patterson as its chairman, to discuss the idea with the Committee on the Library of Congress. Since Congress had recently appropriated $180,000 to enlarge the space of its library, Henry was confident that the accommodations were "sufficient for all our books and the annual increase of both libraries during the next fifteen years." The shelves of the west wing were, by contrast, "filled to overflowing," and as a precaution against fire, the west wing could not even be heated during the winter. The fireproof confines of the Library of Congress looked inviting indeed by comparison.[22]

The committee reported back to the regents in late February, recommending that the books be placed in the Library of Congress on condition that the public have access to the collection on weekdays, and that the Secretary and his staff would have the same privileges as any member of Congress. In March 1866, Congressman Patterson introduced into the House legislation that would allow the Librarian of Congress to employ two additional assistants, and appropriated five hundred dollars to defray the expenses of transferring the books. The bill received quick approval, and was signed by President Andrew Johnson. Secretary Henry, who had fought so hard against Jewett over a decade before, had mixed feelings about the departure of the volumes. "If all things were equal, I would prefer to retain our Library within our own building, yet in the actual condition of affairs I think the transfer will be beneficial not only to the Institution but also to the public." Within a year he discerned a new "spirit of pride in the Library of Congress which will serve to make it a collection of books worthy of the Capital of the nation. . . . Already the proposition had been suggested to erect a separate building for the exclusive use of the Library." Henry felt in no small part responsible for this and predicted to Asa Gray that in "time a similar result will be produced in regard to the museum."[23]

The great unfinished business of the renovation of the Castle was the question of the best use for the large room on the second floor of the main building, which remained an empty shell. At the annual meeting of the regents in 1868, a special committee observed that the "policy which has led to the transfer of the Smithsonian library to that of Congress suggests the propriety of severing also the museum from the Smithsonian Institution, inasmuch as a museum is no more contemplated by the will of Smithson than a library." The Institution had amassed in the library the "most complete collection of learned transactions in existence," acquired by means of exchange for the Smithsonian Contributions to Knowledge series, and the committee proposed to make the collections of the museum just as complete by instituting a similar exchange policy for specimens of natural history. The obvious use for the second story, "and such other rooms as are not required for the regular operations of the institution," was office and display space for the "scientific collections."[24]

The regents appointed another committee to estimate the size of the appropriation to be requested from "Congress for the care of the museum and for fitting up the great hall for the safe-keeping and exhibition of specimens." On April 22, 1868, the committee suggested that "$50,000 would be required for finishing the large room and supplying it with cases, and that at least $10,000 annually ought to be appropriated for the care of the museum." The regents concluded that a memorial should be sent to Congress, and so one was on May first. They reminded that august body of the cost "of so large and expensive an edifice," and the "grievous burden" which the museum placed upon the Smithsonian. The $4,000 appropriated since the days of the Patent Office "scarcely more than defrays, at the present time, one-third of the annual expense." The regents announced their unwillingness "to embarass the active operations for several years to come, by devoting a large part of the income" to fitting up the large hall for the display of the specimens of the government, concluding instead "to allow this room to remain unfinished until other means are provided for completing it."

It was not, the memorial continued, "by its castellated building nor the exhibition of the museum of the government that the Institution has achieved its present reputation. . . . It is by its explorations, its researches, its publications, its distribution of specimens and its exchanges, constituting . . . an active, living organization, that it has rendered itself favorably known in every part of the civilized world." Although $12,000 had been spent on specimens in 1867, the regents asked for $10,000 for that purpose and another $25,000 "towards the completion of the hall required for the government collections." [25]

Congress, for its part, was unimpressed, and appropriated only $4,000. The regents voted in January 1869 to "renew their application to Congress to increase the annual appropriation for the care of the government collections to $10,000." The new entreaty did as much good as the old, for in May 1870 the regents found themselves once again resolving to apply to Congress for support of the museum. The third annual memorial apparently persuaded Congress to act, for the Secretary announced to the regents in January 1871 "that Congress has appropriated $10,000 for the care of the Government collections," and that they had "also appropriated $10,000 toward the completion of the upper hall." The Secretary of the Interior, through whom the funds were channeled, appointed Edward Clark, the Architect of the Capitol, to oversee the work. By May, Henry could write to John Torrey that the workmen are making good progress in the work on the building and I hope before the next session of Congress we shall be able to make a good display." Thousands of specimens were being "constantly received," but Henry still worried that the reputation of the Institution suffered "from the unsightly appearance of the Museum. The architecture of the room in which the articles are deposited is unfitted for the objects and the articles themselves are not in all cases of a character to please the public eye. Museums, to be effective as a means of adult education, must be attractive, and the articles of purely scientific interest put away in drawers for special exhibition." [26]

The large exhibit hall of the second story was furnished by January 1872, and the Secretary could write of "very extensive . . . improvements in the building." The west wing was finally fireproofed, and the basement at that end of the building was fitted up as a work room for natural history. In the east end of the basement was placed the chemical laboratory which had formerly been one floor up, in the east wing. The first floor of the east wing and the east range were converted into offices for the "active operations of the Institution," including exchanges. The new arrangement segregated Spencer Baird (fig. 37) and his natural history staff into the west end,

Figure 37. Spencer F. Baird, Assistant Secretary for the Museum.

and the Secretary and "all the business of the Smithsonian proper to the east wing. By this change," Henry wrote, "all the bad smells which annoy my family will be avoided and I shall be able to show how small a space is sufficient to carry on the legitimate operations of the establishment."[27] Henry saw the internal arrangements as a way of expressing the difference between the "legitimate operations" and the museum function, a difference he hoped was not lost upon the Congress.

Baird was able to extract from Congress a deficiency appropriation of $5,000 to convert the west wing into a mineralogical museum, which would receive the collection of the Department of the Interior. By March 1873, Henry exultantly wrote to Asa Gray that "Congress has at length come into the measure which I have so long advocated of making an annual appropriation for the full support of the national museum. At the session which just closed it appropriated upwards of $40,000 for the care of the museum, the fitting up [of] the rooms and the beginning of heating arrangements."[28]

At the annual meeting of the regents in January 1873, Henry suggested that the regents consider depositing the "articles of fine art belonging to the Institution in the Corcoran Art Gallery," and the Executive Committee was ordered to look into the matter. In February the Committee reported that Corcoran intended his gallery to be "one of very high order of art, and, with some exceptions he specified, he is of the opinion the specimens of the Smithsonian will not come within the scope of his design." Henry was not one to be so easily put off, and by the next annual meeting of the regents, the Secretary had been elected a trustee of the Corcoran Gallery. He told the assembled regents that "it was proper that some of the articles now in the building should be deposited in the Corcoran Gallery, subject, of course, to the order of the Regents." The regents, of course, followed the wishes of their Secretary and authorized him to deposit "such works of art belonging to the Institution as may be approved by the executive committee." Before the year was out, Henry had accomplished his purpose.[29]

In January 1875, a special committee of regents was appointed to examine the museum. Asa Gray, who had replaced the late Louis Agassiz on the board, lavished praise on the ethnological and archaeological exhibits housed in the large exhibit hall on the second story of the main building: "It is a great pleasure to see how well cared for and how important this museum is, and how much it interests a numerous throng of visitors. In this respect it seems likely to be even more attractive than the museum of natural history underneath." Gray observed that the museum was "very rapidly increasing, and it is remarkable that the accessions are made almost without pecuniary cost." The most rapid increases, however, were in the planning stages, and were to flood over Secretary Henry's "active operations."[30]

Since early 1874, a board consisting of representatives from the various branches of the federal government had been making preparations for a collective exhibition at the Centennial Exhibition of 1876 to be held in Philadelphia. Spencer Baird represented both the Smithsonian and the United States Fish Commission. Among Baird's plans for the Centennial was a large glass-topped refrigerator which was to be "stocked every day with various fishes from all portions of the United States." At the end of each day, the fish would be taken to restaurants on the grounds, where hungry fairgoers could consume what they had seen.

Joseph Henry probably wished that more of the exhibits were edible, for although ethnological displays had been left to the Indian Bureau, a "large force of taxidermists" were at work in the Castle preparing the natural history exhibit. Having been displayed in Philadelphia, the exhibits would "all be brought back to Washington, where, with proper facilities to be furnished by Congress, [they] will be displayed to interested visitors, it is hoped for centuries to come." Where they would be shown in Washington was another matter. Baird observed in his January 1876 report on the Centennial "that the Smithsonian Building will be entirely inadequate to accommodate this collection on its return from Philadelphia, especially as even now it is overcrowded and packed from top to bottom with thousands of boxes, for the proper exhibition of which there is no space or opportunity at the present time."[31]

Secretary Henry wrote to Asa Gray that the January 1876 meeting of the Board of Regents "will be one of importance and matters may be discussed which will have an influence on the future history of the establishment. The great increase in the number of specimens in the Museum, consequent on the Centennial Exposition, will necessitate a much larger building for their accommodation than the present Smithsonian edifice." Henry was undecided as to whether the new building should be "an extension of the present Smithsonian edifice or a separate one; or one in connection with the Library of Congress." He was becoming more and more convinced of the advisability of separating the Smithsonian from the National Museum, in light of the latter's stupendous growth and subsequent dependence on federal appropriations, which in turn required extensive lobbying. The meeting of which the Secretary expected so much resulted only in the appointment of another special committee "to take into consideration the connection of the Smithsonian Institution and the National Museum, and to recommend such action as may be thought proper in relation to the matter."[32]

By December 1876, Henry had decided that "when the separation takes place it ought to be with the condition that the Government take charge of the present Smithsonian building." And the best way to insure that the government would buy the Castle was to insist that any new building for the National Museum be adjacent if not adjoining the Smithsonian Building. The need for more room had intensified even further when almost all of the foreign countries represented at the Centennial, as well as a number of states, gave their exhibits to the National Museum. This forced Congress to grant the Smithsonian use of the dilapidated pre–Civil War Armory Building to the east of the Castle on the Mall. There the collections would be stored until more permanent accommodations were ready. Legislation was introduced in Congress "for the erection of a building to contain . . . the National Museum," and Secretary Henry felt that a "sharp look-out has therefore to be kept to prevent this building being separated from the present Smithsonian edifice." He planned to lobby for the "appropriation for the new building and also for placing it in the rear of the present edifice, taking care at the same time to remind Congress that the present building belongs to the Smithsonian fund and ought to be repaid."[33]

General Montgomery Meigs, who had superintended the extension of the United States Capitol in the 1850s was the probable architect of a plan for a National Museum that would form a "wing adjoining [the] old South tower" (fig. 38). The resultant proposal attempted to be at least minimally compatible with the style of the original building, without actually being in the Norman style. In this it closely followed Adolph Cluss's Department of Agriculture Building of 1868, which was situated west of the Castle on the Mall. Although the Agriculture Building had been inspired by the Second Empire design of James Renwick, Jr., for the Corcoran Gallery of Art of 1859, Cluss related the Agriculture Building to the Smithsonian in several ways. The predominant use of red brick gave the building a similar color; molding between brick piers hazily suggested the corbel coursing of the Castle; and five large rounded-head windows dominated the central section of the Agriculture Building.[34]

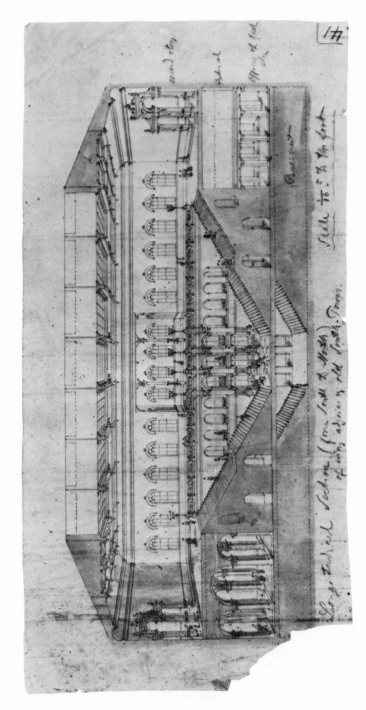

Figure 38. *Montgomery Meigs, Proposed wing, Smithsonian Building. ca. 1877.*

The proposed wing of the Castle was also to have been of red brick, though what was the mansard roof of the Agriculture Building became in the plan for the wing a simple hipped roof. The large windows of the second floor of the new wing were to strongly resemble those of Agriculture. On both a rounded arch was visually reinforced with molding, and on both two vertical muntins rose to form an arch and thus echo the wider arch of the entire window. While maintaining the more classical feel of the Agriculture Building, the rounded-arch windows would have harmonized as well with those of the main building of the Castle.

The core of the wing was a grand stairway, with two staircases descending from the north and south ends of the second floor to the center of the first floor. Landings half way down opened onto a mezzanine floor. This floor did not extend to the south end of the wing, where a grand entrance way, lined with large columns supporting a groined-arch ceiling, rose all the way to the floor of the second story. The outsized columns and the vast central space, with its balustrades on the mezzanine and second stories, anticipated Meigs's 1883 design for the Pension Building in Washington.

The likelihood of congressional approval for a separate museum building increased when Senator Justin Morrill of Vermont became interested in the plight of the National Museum. Morrill objected, however, to the idea of a large wing because the new addition would crown the site and interfere with the carriage ways on the Mall. Baird, who as Henry had observed was "much interested in having the two buildings united," had to give up the "idea of placing the new one in the rear" of the Castle. Meigs set to work on a new plan, a one-story, utilitarian edifice to be placed between the Castle and the Agriculture Department.[35]

Secretary Henry fully approved of the Meigs design, writing that the building would "be of durable though inexpensive material, and expressly adapted to the uses for which it is designed"—unlike, he implied, certain sandstone castles. Henry emphasized that the "great object of interest" was to be the inside and not the outside. "Due attention, however, will be given to the aesthetical part of the structure though this will be subordinate to the useful. It will have at least the beauty of *adaptation* to the purposes for which it is intended."[36]

Although he remained confident that the National Museum and

Figure 39. Adolph Cluss and Paul Schulze, United States National Museum Building, now the Arts and Industries Building. 1879.

the Smithsonian would become separate entities, a doubt finally appeared in Henry's mind that he might not be able to persuade Congress to buy the Castle. A new building, he reasoned, would allow for the removal of all the specimens from the Smithsonian Building; perhaps the empty space could accommodate the "signal service operation and the display of the objects of the educational department, [with the] government paying the Institution a rent for the space occupied." At long last Henry recognized that it would be "very difficult to disassociate the Institution from the present building with which it has been so long connected." Despite his admission that the Castle had become the public symbol for the Smithsonian Institution, his plan to lease its rooms reaffirmed his dogged belief that the Smithsonian was not a museum, and that it did not need such a large building.[37]

The Secretary's meditations on ridding himself of the museum were, it turned out, premature. Senator Morrill had duly introduced legislation to appropriate $250,000 for the realization of Meigs's plan, and then managed the bill through the Senate with little opposition. A technicality bottled up the bill in the House of Representatives, however, and it never even came to a vote. The issue died for the year.

Another attempt was made early in 1878, but Secretary Henry, now eighty years of age, had been taken ill the previous autumn and "was able to bestow but little attention to the details of the work of the Institution." Not until March 1879 did the $250,000 appropriation for a new building finally pass the Congress. Montgomery Meigs and Edward Clark, the Architect of the Capitol, approved plans by Adolph Cluss and his new partner, Paul Schulze, for a National Museum Building (fig. 39). The red brick structure with polychromatic trim was to be everything that the Castle had not been: fireproof, leakproof, inexpensive, and planned with one specific function in mind, a museum.[38] The Secretary of the Smithsonian no longer agitated for the separation of the National Museum, however. That was because the Secretary of the Institution was now Spencer F. Baird. Joseph Henry had died the year before, in May of 1878.

Envoi

❧

WHEN Joseph Henry breathed his last, his Smithsonian Institution died with him. Henry, in his commitment to scientific research, had denied the validity of other interpretations of Smithson's will: to Henry the Smithsonian was not a library, not an art gallery, not a museum. Spencer F. Baird, Henry's successor, had no intention of curtailing the Institution's efforts at increasing knowledge through original research, but neither did he have the least intention of giving up the museum.

The spatial presence of the Castle chained Joseph Henry to the United States National Museum, and ensured that Henry would not be able to completely thwart the legislative intent of the original Smithsonian bill. Robert Dale Owen had provided in his bill for a wide variety of functions which the Institution would perform; Henry, looking back to the will of Smithson to justify his evasion of congressional intent, succeeded in dealing away all of the functions except the museum. As long as the Smithsonian possessed a spacious building such as the Castle, the Congress could see no reason for another cultural institution, despite Henry's ferocious insistence that a museum was an "improper" application of the Smithson bequest. If Robert Dale Owen had not guided the Castle to an advanced stage of construction, Henry could have refused to spend the bequest on a building, and most likely would have had his way, concerning both the building and the Institution.

Under Spencer Baird and the following Secretaries, the other functions gradually crept back into the Institution. The Smithsonian of today, the network of museums, art galleries, libraries, and scientific research centers, reflect the broadly conceived intentions of Robert Dale Owen rather than the more specialized vision of Joseph Henry. Owen's Castle forced upon Henry a far different Institution from the one he so strongly advocated.

Abbreviations

JH   Joseph Henry
HH   Harriet Henry
ADB   Alexander Dallas Bache
RDO   Robert Dale Owen
JH-HH   Joseph Henry-Harriet Henry Correspondence, 1825–1878, Joseph Henry Papers, Smithsonian Institution Archives, Record Unit 7001.
JH-ADB   Joseph Henry-Alexander Dallas Bache Correspondence, 1834–1867, Smithsonian Institution Archives, Record Unit 7001.
JHPP   Joseph Henry Private Papers, Smithsonian Institution Archives, Record Unit 7001.
ADBP   Alexander Dallas Bache Papers, Private Correspondence, Smithsonian Institution Archives, Record Unit 7053.
SIA   Smithsonian Institution Archives.
Rhees, *Journals*   William J. Rhees, *The Smithsonian Institution: Journals of the Board of Regents, Reports of Committees, Etc.* (Washington, D.C., 1879).
Rhees, *Documents* William J. Rhees, *The Smithsonian Institution: Documents Relative to Its Origin and History* (Washington, D.C., 1879).

Notes

Introduction

1. Horatio Greenough, *The Travels, Observations, and Experience of a Yankee Stonecutter* (New York, 1852; A Scholar's Facsimile Reprint, Gainesville, 1958), pp. 44–47.
2. JH to HH, January 26, 1847, JH-HH.

Chapter One

1. Geoffrey T. Hellman, *The Smithsonian: Octopus on the Mall* (Philadelphia, 1967), pp. 37–50; Rhees, *Documents*, pp. 3–133.
2. On Town, Davis and Dakin, see Jane B. Davies, "A. J. Davis' Projects for a Patent Office Building, 1832–34," *Journal of the Society of Architectural Historians* XXIV:3 (October 1965), and "Six Letters by William P. Elliot to Alexander J. Davis, 1834–1838, *Journal of the Society of Architectural Historians* XXVI:1 (March 1967), pp. 71–73; for the actual Patent Office, see Louise Hall, "The Design of the Old Patent Office," *Journal of the Society of Architectural Historians* XV:1 (March 1956), pp. 27–30, and Wilcomb E. Washburn, "Temple of the Arts," *American Institute of Architects Journal* (March 1969). My account of the Davis project is drawn from the Davies article.
3. The Davis project for the Smithsonian Institution is at the Metropolitan Museum of Art, New York.
4. On Washington architecture, see Daniel D. Reiff, *Washington Architecture 1791–1861: Problems in Development* (Washington, D.C., 1971); on the Patent Office, Davies, "Davis' Projects," p. 231.
5. On Smirke, Wilkins, and the English scene, see Sir John Summerson, *Architecture in Britain, 1530–1830* (Middlesex, 1953, 5th rev. ed. 1969), chap. 29. On Wilkins, see R. W. Liscombe, *William Wilkins* (Cambridge, 1980), particularly pls. 84 and 85.
6. Elliot is quoted in Davies, "Six Letters"; on Mills in Washington, see Reiff, *Washington Architecture*, pp. 35–41.
7. A. Hunter Dupree, *Science in the Federal Government* (Cambridge, Mass., 1957), p. 70; Herbert Everett Putnam, *Joel Roberts Poinsett: A Political Biography*

158 *Notes*

(Washington, D.C., 1967), pp. 196–97.

8. On Mills and Latrobe, see Talbot F. Hamlin, *Benjamin Henry Latrobe* (New York, 1955), pp. 344–46. Mills's reading list is found in Mills to RDO, undated, in the South Carolina Historical Society, reprinted in H. M. P. Gallagher, *Robert Mills* (New York, 1935), p. 194. My thanks to Professor John Morrill Bryan of the University of South Carolina, who sent me a photocopy of the original letter.

9. The Mills quotation is from Gallagher; on New York University, see Arthur Scully, Jr., *James Dakin, Architect* (Baton Rouge, 1973), pp. 18–22; on Mills's Washington Jail, see James M. Goode, *Capital Losses: A Cultural History of Washington's Destroyed Buildings* (Washington, D.C., 1979), pp. 304–305.

10. Various elevations and a first-floor plan for Mills's Smithsonian project are in the Cartographic Division of the National Archives.

11. The Mills quotation on buttresses is from Gallagher, *Mills*.

12. Dupree, *Science in the Federal Government*, pp. 70ff.

13. Rhees, *Documents*, pp. 262–65, 302–351.

14. Richard Rush to Francis Markoe, March 4, 1842, National Institute Records, RU 7058, SIA; Cheesman A. Herrick, *History of Girard College* (Philadelphia, 1927), pp. 1–33, 171–83; "Nicholas Biddle and the Architecture of Girard College," *The Pennsylvania Magazine of History and Biography* XVIII (October 1894), pp. 354–60.

15. Rhees, *Documents*, pp. 303–305.

16. Rhees, *Documents*, pp. 307, 167–69. See also Wilcomb E. Washburn's introduction to John Quincy Adams, *The Great Design* (Washington, D.C., 1965), especially p. 15.

17. George Perkins Marsh, *The Goths in New England* (Middlebury, 1843), p. 26.

18. John King Lord, *A History of Dartmouth College, 1815–1908* (Concord, 1913), pp. 132–35; *Catalogue of the Private Library of the Late Hon. Rufus Choate* (Boston, 1859).

19. Rhees, *Documents*, pp. 334, 350.

20. The standard biography is Richard William Leopold, *Robert Dale Owen* (Cambridge, Mass., 1940). Much of this paragraph is drawn from Robert Dale Owen, *Threading My Way: Twenty-seven Years of Autobiography* (New York, 1874), especially pp. 177–78, 180, and 120, where Owen writes of Scott's works: ". . . what sunny memories, what hours of rapt enjoyment, do the very titles still call up!" On the influence of Hofwyl in America, see Joseph M. Hawes, *Children in Urban Society* (New York, 1971), pp. 30–32.

21. Arthur Bestor, *Backwoods Utopias* (Philadelphia, 1950), pp. 76, 128; information in caption of engraved illustration (see fig. 3); Owen, in *Threading My Way* (p. 263), relates that Stedman Whitwell was a "convert to my father's views," and actually made the trip to New Harmony.

22. Leopold, *Owen*, pp. 47–64, 82, 157–58, 220.

23. Rhees, *Documents*, pp. 355–56.

24. Rhees, loc. cit.

25. This paragraph and the next are based on Rhees, *Documents*, pp. 366–67, 374–75, 379–80, and 384.

26. Rhees, *Documents*, pp. 426.

27. Rhees, *Documents*, pp. 467–73.

28. Rhees, *Documents*, p. 469, compared with index in *Congressional Globe* for Twenty-ninth Congress. My decision to break down the vote by three categories instead of a simple north-south came only after I had tabulated the results from each state delegation. A. Hunter Dupree, *Science in the Federal Government*, p. 79, notes the strange alliance of Thomas Hart Benton and John C. Calhoun on their vote against the Smithsonian bill in the Senate. Jacksonians had two reasons for voting against the bill: opposition to anything remotely resembling a corporation, or the removal of most of the populist measures in the bill. Owen voted for the bill, even though his pet provision, the normal school, had been excised. Incidentally, the *Congressional Globe* list of yeas and nays on the House vote should tally 85–75, not 85–76 as printed.

29. Rhees, *Journals*, p. 1.

30. RDO to Richard Rush, August 16, 1846, Richard Rush Papers, Smithson Bequest, Princeton University Library.

31. RDO to David Dale Owen, August 15, 1845, in David Henry Arnot, *Animadversions on the Proceedings of the Regents of the Smithsonian Institution in Their Choice of an Architect* (New York, 1847), p. 7; Robert Mills to RDO, in Gallagher, *Mills*, pp. 193, 198.

32. RDO, David Dale Owen, in Arnot, *Animadversions*.

33. David Dale Owen, in Arnot, *Animadversions*.

34. David Dale Owen's plan for the Smithsonian is described in great detail in his letter to Robert Dale Owen, October 10, 1845, Workingmen's Institute, New Harmony, Indiana.

35. On cast iron architecture, see Henry-Russell Hitchcock, *Architecture: Nineteenth and Twentieth Centuries*, 4th ed. (Middlesex, 1977), chap. 7.

36. See note 30, above.

Chapter Two

1. Weather report from James K. Polk, *Diary*, ed. Milo Milton Quaife (Chicago, 1910), p. 120; Rhees, *Journals*, pp. 1–2.

2. For Totten, see the *Dictionary of American Biography*; Albert E. Cowdrey, *A City for the Nation* (Washington, D.C., 1978), pp. 15–17; R. Ernest Dupuy, *Where They Have Trod: The West Point Tradition in American Life* (New York, 1940), pp. 178–79.

3. Merle Odgers, *Alexander Dallas Bache: Scientist and Educator* (Philadelphia, 1947), pp. 12, 15–16, 32, 61, 63, 96; Varina Davis, *Jefferson Davis, A Memoir* (New York, 1890), p. 262.

4. Odgers, *Bache*.

5. Rhees, *Journals*, pp. 2–3.

6. Polk, *Diary*, pp. 124–25; National Capitol Planning Commission, *Worthy of the Nation*, ed. Frederick A. Gutheim (Washington, D.C., 1977), pp. 57, 79, 101.

7. *National Intelligencer*, August 28, 1846.

8. Isaiah Rogers, *Diary*, p. 529, transcribed by Denys Peter Myers, original in Avery Library, Columbia University.

9. Rhees, *Journals*, p. 4.

10. Rogers, *Diary*, loc. cit.

11. James Renwick, Sr., to ADB, September 8, 1846, ADBP, Private Correspondence, Box 3, SIA.

12. RDO to Richard Rush, September 10, 1846, Richard Rush Papers, Smithson Bequest, Princeton University Library; Rhees, *Journals*, p. 6; Thomas U. Walter to ADB, December 11, 1846, ADBP.

13. Rhees, *Journals*, p. 6; RDO to Rush, September 10, 1846.

14. Rhees, *Journals*, p. 6; Rogers, *Diary*, p. 532; RDO to ADB, September 22, 1846, ADBP.

15. For years the best published account of Renwick's life was Talbot Hamlin's entry in the *Dictionary of American Biography*; this has now been supplemented by a solid chapter in William H. Pierson, Jr., *American Buildings and Their Architects*, vol. II-A (Garden City, 1978), chap. 5. One must reconsider Pierson's assertion that "Renwick was born in New York City to a socially prominent family of comfortable means. His mother was Margaret Brevoort, the daughter of a cultured, well-established New York family." (p. 216). For a remarkably different view, see *The Autobiography of Rear Admiral Charles Wilkes, U.S. Navy 1798–1877*, ed. W. J. Morgan et al. (Washington, D.C., 1978), p. 725; the bankruptcy notice of James Renwick, Sr., is in the Renwick Family Papers, Special Collections, Columbia University Library.

16. The senior Renwick's watercolors are in the Special Collections of Columbia University Library. The school of Palladio quotation is from James Renwick, Sr., to Edward Sabine, October 30, 1849, Edward Sabine Papers, BJ3/49, Records of Kew Observatory, Public Record Office, London; on the senior Renwick's Gothic plan for Columbia, see Adolf Plàczek, *Journal of the Society of Architectural Historians* XI (May 1952), pp. 22–23. Washington Irving enjoyed taking his visitors to England along the route of the first canto of Sir Walter Scott's *The Lady of the Lake*. See *The Reminiscences of William Campbell Preston*, ed. Minnie Clare Yarborough (Chapel Hill, 1933), pp. 42–46.

17. For Henry Renwick, see the *Dictionary of American Biography*. He served on the United States Boundary Commission for several years. For Edward Renwick, see the DAB and his biographical memoir in *The Renwicks*, compiled by James Adolf Leftwich (New York, 1946), p. 27, in the Local History and Genealogy Division, the New York Public Library. On Jervis, see Larry D. Lankton, *The "Practicable" Engineer: John B. Jervis and the Old Croton Aqueduct* (Chicago, 1977), p. 23; and *The Reminiscences of John B. Jervis*, ed. Neal Fitzsimmons (Syracuse, 1971), pp. 79–80.

18. Philip Hone, *Diary*, ed. Bayard Tuckerman (New York, 1889), vol. II, p. 85. For some reason, Allan Nevins edited Hone's estimate of the farm's value out of his edition. *Wilkes*, ed. Morgan et al., p. 725; George Templeton Strong, *Diary*, eds. Allan Nevins and Milton Thomas (New York, 1952), pp. 292–93.

19. William R. Stewart, *Grace Church and Old New York* (New York, 1924), pp. 129–31.

20. See Pierson, *American Buildings*, pp. 215–17.

21. Stewart, *Grace Church*, pp. 152–56, 159–63.

22. Stewart, pp. 158–59. The wooden steeples remained until 1883. Strong, *Diary*, p. 256; Philip Hone, *Diary*, ed. Allan Nevins (New York, 1936), p. 754.

23. RDO, *Hints on Public Architecture* (New York, 1849; reprint ed. New York, 1978, with an introduction by Cynthia R. Field), p. 96; Stewart, *Grace Church*, p. 138; Pierson, *American Buildings*, pp. 217–18.

24. Samuel M. Shoemaker, *Calvary Church, Yesterday and Today* (New York, 1936), p. 54; *New York Post*, August 6, 1847, quoted in Shoemaker, p. 54; Pierson, *American Buildings*, pp. 218–19; on McVicar see Phoebe B. Stanton, *The Gothic Revival and American Church Architecture* (Baltimore, 1968), pp. 68–69, 160; Jay E. Cantor, "The Public Architecture of James Renwick, Jr." Master's thesis, University of Delaware, 1967, p. 18.

25. Strong, *Diary*, pp. 464–65.

26. The following account is based on Rhees, *Journals*, pp. 6–9, 441.

Chapter Three

1. Francis Markoe to Richard Rush, August 19, 1846, Richard Rush Papers, Smithson Bequest, Princeton University Library.

2. Thomas Coulson, *Joseph Henry: His Life and Works* (Princeton, 1950), is the standard biography. See also *The Papers of Joseph Henry*, ed. Nathan Reingold (Washington, D.C., 1972—), and Wilcomb E. Washburn, "Joseph Henry's Conception of the Purpose of the Smithsonian Institution," in *A Cabinet of Curiosities*, ed. Walter Muir Whitehill (Charlottesville, 1967), pp. 133ff.

3. This and the following two paragraphs are based on JH to ADB, September 6, 1846, ADBP.

4. JH to Bullions, October 14, 1846, and JH to Amos Dean, October 19, 1846, JHPP; JH to James Henry, December 2, 1846, JH Family Correspondence, 1825–1877, SIA.

5. Markoe to Rush, October 13, 1846, Richard Rush Papers, Smithson Bequest, Princeton University Library.

6. Rhees, *Journals*, pp. 10–13.

7. Rhees, *Journals*, pp. 10–13. On Pickering, see A. Hunter Dupree, *Science in the Federal Government* (Cambridge, Mass., 1957), pp. 73–74.

8. ADB to JH, December 4, 1846, Rare Book Collection, University of Pennsylvania.

9. Rhees, *Journals*, p. 13.

10. Rhees, *Journals*, p. 13, and ADB to JH, December 5, 1846, JH-ADB. Bache's whimsical description of his uncle was no exaggeration. Varina Davis recalled that Dallas's "snowy white" hair "was inclined to curl," and that "there was a certain nice, delicate sense of harmony and propriety about everything he did." Dallas was thus eminently qualified for the rigors of the vice-presidency. See Varina Davis, *Jefferson Davis, A Memoir* (New York, 1890), p. 268.

11. JH to Asa Gray, December 12, 1846, Gray Herbarium, Harvard University.

12. Charles Lyell, *Travels in North America, in the Years 1841–2* (New York, 1845), vol. I, p. 89.

13. JH to HH, January 20, 1847, JH-HH.

14. Thomas U. Walter to ADB, December 11, 1846, ADBP. On Walter and Bache, see Merle M. Odgers, *Alexander Dallas Bache*, p. 96. On Walter and Biddle, see above, chap. 1, note 14.

15. JH to HH, December 15 and December 18, 1846, JH-HH.

16. JH to HH, December 20, 1846, JH-HH.

17. JH to HH, December 21, 1846, JH-HH.

18. Rhees, *Journals*, p. 18.

19. Rhees, *Journals*, pp. 9, 16–17, 19; James K. Polk, *Diary*, ed. M. M. Quaife (Chicago, 1910), pp. 264–65, 272–73, 284.

20. Isaiah Rogers, *Diary*, pp. 532, 548, transcribed by Denys Peter Myers, original in Avery Library, Columbia University.

21. Howard Daniels designed the Greek mode Montgomery County Courthouse in Dayton, Ohio. See Talbot F. Hamlin, *Greek Revival Architecture in America* (New York, 1944), p. 286, and Neville H. Clouten, "The Old Montgomery County Court House, Dayton, Ohio," *Journal of the Society of Architectural Historians* XXVI (December 1967), especially p. 299. The competition entries of Notman, Warren, and the east elevation of Rogers's design are in the Smithsonian Institution Archives.

Renwick's original competition entries have not been uncovered; SIA has north and south elevations for the Norman plan, in watercolor, of uncertain date. The floor plan and various perspective views of the Norman and Gothic plans may be found in Robert Dale Owen, *Hints on Public Architecture* (New York, 1849; reprint ed. New York, 1978). All these views show the exterior of the two-story building, but the evidence laid out in the succeeding pages strongly suggests that Renwick's original Norman plan, and perhaps his Gothic plan, were *three* stories tall, like the Owen plan and like most of the other competitors, and cut down to two main stories by the Board of Regents.

The style of designs by Arnot and Haviland are hinted at by Owen in his preparations for *Hints*. Owen wanted two plates of Renwick's Norman design, and one each of Renwick's Gothic plan, the "Norman plan submitted by Mr. Haviland," either Arnot's or Notman's, and the "Italian plan submitted by Mr. Daniel [sic]" (Rhees, *Journals*, pp. 671–72). Owen obviously wanted one illustration of each style submitted, and Arnot's, like Notman's, must have been Gothic. It certainly wasn't Norman, for, as we shall see, Arnot later blasted the "barbarism" of the style chosen.

22. Rogers, *Diary*, p. 551.

23. Luther Bradish to Gideon Hawley, and Luther Bradish to Daniel Webster, both dated December 26, 1846, Luther Bradish Papers, courtesy of the New-York Historical Society, New York City.

24. Rogers, *Diary*, p. 550.

25. Rogers, *Diary*, p. 551.

26. Rogers, *Diary*, pp. 552–53. Rogers had been among the architects who gathered at the Astor House in New York City on December 6, 1836, to found an architectural society, which foundered for some twenty years before it was revitalized as the American Institute of Architects.

27. JH to HH, January 16, 1847, JH-HH.

28. JH to HH, January 18, 1847, JH-HH. This letter makes clear that Renwick had "cut down" part of his building, most likely the third story, and preserved the wings.

29. JH to HH, January 19 and 20, 1847, JH-HH.

30. JH to HH, January 20, 1847, JH-HH.

31. Rhees, *Journals*, pp. 20, 21.

32. Rhees, *Journals*, loc. cit.

33. Rhees, *Journals*, loc. cit.; JH to HH, January 20, 1847, JH-HH.

34. Rhees, *Journals*, pp. 22–23; Rogers, *Diary*, p. 554. On William Archer, see Rhees, *Journals*, pp. 4–5, 690, and also James M. Goode, *Capital Losses: A Cultural History of Washington's Destroyed Buildings* (Washington, D.C., 1979), pp. 195–96.

35. Rhees, *Journals*, pp. 23–24; JH to HH, January 23, 1847, JH-HH.

36. Rhees, *Journals*, pp. 23–24.

37. Rhees, *Journals*, loc. cit.

38. JH to HH, January 26, 1847, JH-HH. Henry noted that his side was weaker with the departure of Rush, but Rush's letter excusing himself also expresses a preference for Renwick's plan. Either the letter was not read aloud or Henry was otherwise occupied.

39. Rhees, *Journals*, p. 29; JH to HH, January 27, 1846, JH-HH.

40. Rhees, *Journals*, p. 29; Rogers, *Diary*, p. 555; JH to HH, January 30, 1847, JH-HH.

41. Rogers, *Diary*, p. 556. David Arnot, *Animadversions on the Proceedings of the Regents of the Smithsonian Institution in Their Choice of an Architect* (New York, 1847), p. 13, quotes a petition signed by Arnot, Wells, Notman, and Rogers, claiming that the "full extent of our labors has not been taken into sufficient account by the honorable members of your Board, and [the architects] therefore beg a more careful consideration of our respective claims."

42. Rhees, *Journals*, pp. 31–36; George Templeton Strong, *Diary*, eds. Allan Nevins and Milton Thomas (New York, 1952), p. 288.

43. Arnot, *Animadversions*, pp. 11, 14–15.

44. Rhees, *Journals*, pp. 32–33, 35–36.

Chapter Four

1. JH to HH, March 15, 1847, JH-HH. This letter in SIA is catalogued as "ca. January 1847," but reference in the letter to Mrs. Allen's funeral corresponds to the *National Intelligencer* of March 15, 1847.

2. Rhees, *Journals*, pp. 626, 591, 622.

3. Rhees, *Journals*, p. 622; Samuel Shoemaker, *Calvary Church, Yesterday and Today* (New York, 1936), p. 54.

4. Rhees, *Journals*, p. 627.

5. Rhees, *Journals*, pp. 661, 612, 667. On the Seneca Quarry, see Paul H. Douglas and William K. Jones, "Sandstone, Canals and the Smithsonian," *The Smithsonian Journal of History* III:1 (Spring 1968), pp. 41–58. Wilcomb E. Washburn first informed me of the existence of this article, and James M. Goode actually found it for me; my thanks go to both of them. Daniel D. Reiff, in *Washington Architecture 1791–1861: Problems in Development* (Washington, D.C., 1971), p. 94, erroneously assumes that lilac gray sandstone is lighter than red sandstone, and thus is forced to say that it "is not certain when the change to the darker red Seneca sandstone . . . was made, but it was well after the foundation of the building had been started." In *Hints on Public Architecture*, published after the completion of the east wing, Owen still refers to the "New Red Sandstone formation . . . such, for example, as the lilac gray variety, used for the Smithsonian building" (p. 99).

6. Rhees, *Journals*, pp. 670, 672, 676, 692.

7. JH to HH, April 13, 1847, JH-HH; on Owen's presence at the construction site, see JH to ADB, May 27, 1848.

8. JH to HH, May 1 and 3, 1847, JH-HH; Constance McLaughlin Green, *Washington: A History of the Capital 1800–1950* (Princeton, 1962), p. 170; *New York Tribune*, May 4, 1847.

9. This and the following paragraph are drawn from George M. Dallas, *Address Delivered on Occasion of Laying the Corner Stone of the Smithsonian Institution at the City of Washington (Washington, D.C., 1847)*, pp. 5–6; reprinted in Rhees, *Journals*, pp. 684–87.

10. JH to HH, May 1, 1847, JH-HH.

11. Rhees, *Journals*, p. 593; JH to HH, May 3, 1847, JH-HH.

12. JH to ADB, June 25, 1847; JH-ADB; see also JH to William Seaton, June 28, 1847, JHPP.

13. ADB to JH, June 29, 1847, Rare Books Collection, University of Pennsylvania.

14. RDO to ADB, August 5, 1847, ADBP.

15. JH to RDO, August 7, 1847, JHPP.

16. Richard William Leopold, *Robert Dale Owen* (Cambridge, Mass., 1940), pp. 238–40; Charles G. Page to JH, August 14, 1847, JHPP.

17. JH to James Renwick, Jr., August 16, 1847, JHPP.

18. JH to William Campbell Preston, October 14, 1847, JHPP.

19. JH to Asa Gray, January 10, 1848, Gray Herbarium, Harvard University.

20. Rhees, *Journals*, p. 692.

21. Rhees, *Journals*, pp. 40–43.

22. Rhees, *Journals*, pp. 44–45.

23. JH to Asa Gray, January 10, 1848, Gray Herbarium, Harvard University.

24. This and the following paragraph are from Rhees, *Journals*, pp. 45–47.

25. RDO to ADB, December 23, 1847, ADBP. This letter is in SIA marked only as "Thursday morning," but all references pinpoint it to this date. On Owen's head, see Leopold, *Owen*, p. 51.

26. Rhees, *Journals*, pp. 47–49.

27. This and the following paragraph are drawn from JH to William Campbell Preston, February 1, 1848 (copy), JHPP.

28. JH to Jefferson Davis, February 2, 1848, JHPP. See also Varina Davis, *Jefferson Davis, A Memoir* (New York, 1890), pp. 262–63, and *The Papers of Jefferson Davis*, vol. I, eds. Haskell M. Monroe, Jr., and James T. McIntosh (Baton Rouge, 1971), pp. lxxx–lxxxi.

29. JH to Charles C. Jewett, March 8, 1848, JHPP; Leopold, *Owen*, p. 244; *The Papers of Andrew Johnson*, vol. I, eds. Leroy P. Graf and Ralph W. Haskins (Knoxville, 1967), pp. 349–50.

30. This and the following paragraph come from JH to Charles C. Jewett, March 8, 1848, JHPP; and Frank Otto Gatell, *John Gorham Palfrey and the New England Conscience* (Cambridge, Mass., 1963), p. 143. The Whigs now controlled the House but not the Senate.

31. JH to John G. Palfrey, March 31, 1848, JHPP.

32. JH to ADB, March 31, 1848, JH-ADB. On *Moral Physiology*, see Leopold, *Owen*, pp. 78–80.

33. JH to RDO, March 30, 1848, and JH to William Campbell Preston, April 19, 1848, both JHPP.

34. William Campbell Preston to JH, April 30, 1848, JHPP; JH to Asa Gray, May 23, 1848, Gray Herbarium, Harvard University.

35. JH to Asa Gray, May 23, 1848, Gray Herbarium.

36. John Torrey to JH, March 3, 1848, JHPP.

Chapter Five

1. Rhees, *Journals*, pp. 669, 679.

2. See Cynthia R. Field's introduction to the Da Capo reprint edition of *Hints on Public Architecture* (New York, 1978).

3. On Thomas Hope, see two books by David Watkin, *The Rise of Architectural History* (London, 1980), pp. 59–63, and *Thomas Hope 1769–1831 and the Neoclassical Idea* (London, 1968). In the latter work, at p. 145, Watkin defines the *Rundbogenstil* as an amalgam of "features from the Early Christian, Byzantine, Romanesque, and Italian architectures," and discusses Hope's influence upon it.

4. *Hints*, pp. 7, 109.

5. *Hints*, p. 87.

6. Cynthia R. Field, introduction to *Hints*; David Dale Owen to RDO, October 10, 1845, Workingmen's Institute, New Harmony, Indiana.

7. Archibald Alison, *Essays on the Nature and Principles of Taste* (Edinburgh, 1790); George L. Hersey, *High Victorian Gothic: A Study in Associationism* (Baltimore, 1972), pp. 10–14; and Peter Collins, *Changing Ideals in Modern Architecture, 1750–1950* (London and Montreal, 1965).

8. Hersey, pp. 14–22. A biography of Loudon is John Gloag, *Mr. Loudon's England: The Life and Work of John Claudius Loudon and His Influence on Architecture and Furniture Design* (London, 1970).

9. *Hints*, pp. 2, 12.

10. *Hints*, p. 12.

11. *Hints*, pp. 35, 40–41.

12. *Hints*, pp. 47–48.

13. *Hints*, pp. 63, 65, 67.

14. *Hints*, pp. 74–76, 85–90.

15. *Hints*, pp. 85–86.

16. *Hints*, p. 12.

17. *Hints*, pp. 5, 6.

18. Arthur Channing Downs, Jr., generously brought *The Literary World* review to my attention. It appeared in two parts: vol. IV, June 16, 1849, pp. 510–11, and vol. V, July 7, 1849, pp. 4–5. The review is unsigned, but Dr. Downs has pointed out that in an obituary notice of Long on p. 12 of the July 7, 1849, number, Long is cited as the author of a series of papers on architecture and "an occasional poem as well as a review." On Long's writings and architecture, see Phoebe B. Stanton, *The Gothic Revival and American Church Architecture: An Episode in Taste, 1840–1856* (Baltimore, 1968).

19. JH to HH, January 26, 1847, JH-HH; JH to Michael Faraday, June 4, 1851, in L. Pearce Williams, ed., *The Selected Correspondence of Michael Faraday*, vol. II (Cambridge, 1971), pp. 633–34.

20. This and the following paragraph are drawn from Joseph Henry's paper to the American Association for the Advancement of Science, August 22, 1856, "On Acoustics Applied to Public Buildings," in *The Writings of Joseph Henry*, vol. II, Smithsonian Miscellaneous Collections, vol. XXX (Washington, D.C., 1886), pp. 404–406. John Burchard and Albert Bush-Brown briefly discuss Henry's speech in the abridged edition of *The Architecture of America* (Boston, 1966), p. 56.

21. Joseph Henry, "Thoughts on Architecture," an undated essay (ca. 1849), RU 7001, Box 30, Folder 7, JHPP; the essays appears in Arthur P. Molella et al., eds., *A Scientist in American Life: Essays and Lectures of Joseph Henry* (Washington, D.C., 1980), pp. 30–34. The quotation appears on p. 34.

22. Henry, "Thoughts on Architecture," p. 34; Henry, "On Acoustics."

23. *Tenth Annual Report of the Board of Regents of the Smithsonian Institution* (Washington, D.C., 1856), 34th Cong., 2d sess., S. Misc. Doc. 73, p. 15.

24. JH to [ADB?], August 1, 1848, JHPP.

25. Henry, "On Acoustics"; Joseph Henry, "European Diary," entry for April

19, 1837, SIA; JH to Michael Faraday, June 4, 1851, in Williams, *The Selected Correspondence of Michael Faraday*.

Chapter Six

1. JH to ADB, May 11, 1949, JH-ADB.

2. JH to Charles C. Jewett, March 8, 1848, JHPP.

3. JH to Charles C. Jewett, May 19, 1848, JHPP; JH to Asa Gray, May 23, 1848, Gray Herbarium, Harvard University.

4. This and the following two paragraphs are based on JH to ADB, May 27, 1848, JH-ADB.

5. JH to ADB, May 27, 1848, JH-ADB; JH to [ADB?], August 1, 1848, JHPP.

6. Memorial of Joseph Harbaugh and Others, in National Archives RG 233, House of Representatives, 30th Cong., 1845–47, Petitions and Memorials, Committee on Public Buildings and Grounds–Various Subjects (30A G17.1).

7. JH to [ADB?], August 1, 1848, JHPP.

8. Rhees, *Journals*, pp. 695–98.

9. JH to John Torrey, February 18, 1848, marked July 18, 1848, John Torrey Papers, New York Botanical Garden Library; JH to ADB, May 27, 1848, JH-ADB; JH to ADB, May 11, 1849, JH-ADB; Robert Dale Owen, *Hints on Public Architecture* (New York, 1849), p. 105.

10. This and the following three paragraphs are drawn from JH to ADB, May 11, 1849, JH-ADB; Owen, *Hints*; Rhees, *Journals*, p. 699.

11. JH to James A. Pearce, July 21, 1849, JH Desk Diaries, 1849–1865, SIA.

12. JH to Pearce, loc. cit.; JH to George P. Marsh, August 1, 1849, JHPP; JH to ADB, October 23, 1849, JH-ADB.

13. JH to George P. Marsh, August 1, 1849, JHPP; George P. Marsh to JH, August 4, 1849, JHPP. See further information in Wilcomb E. Washburn's essay, "Joseph Henry's Conception of the Purpose of the Smithsonian Institution," in *A Cabinet of Curiosities*, ed. Walter Muir Whitehill (Charlottesville, 1967), pp. 133ff.; see also Rhees, *Journals*, p. 67.

14. This and the following paragraph are from Rhees, *Journals*, pp. 61–66, 699.

15. Rhees, *Journals*, 61–66; John Torrey to JH, April 20, 1850, JHPP.

16. This and the following paragraph are based on Rhees, *Journals*, pp. 64–66, 591–92.

17. Daniel D. Reiff, *Washington Architecture 1791–1861: Problems in Development* (Washington, D.C., 1971), pp. 100–101, 106; James M. Goode, *Capital Losses: A Cultural History of Washington's Destroyed Buildings* (Washington, D.C., 1979), pp. 199–200.

18. Rhees, *Journals*, pp. 75–76, 78–83, 705.

19. Rhees, *Journals*, pp. 83–85.

20. This and the following paragraph are drawn from Rhees, *Journals*, pp. 83–85, and JH Desk Diary, July 29, August 6–7, 1852, SIA.

21. Rhees, *Journals*, p. 707.

Chapter Seven

1. Rhees, *Journals*, pp. 88, 707.

2. James M. Goode, *Capital Losses: A Cultural History of Washington's Destroyed Buildings* (Washington, D.C., 1979), pp. 145–146, 199–201, 305–307.

3. Rhees, *Journals*, pp. 92, 710–11.

4. JH to Richard Rush, July 15, 1853, Richard Rush Papers, Smithson Bequest, Princeton University Library.

5. JH to HH, June 9, 1853, JH-HH; Jefferson Davis to Montgomery C. Meigs, June 7, 1853, *Records of the Office of the Secretary of War*, Letters Sent, vol. 34, p. 310, National Archives, Record Group 107.

6. JH to Mary Henry, June 18, 1853, JH Family Correspondence 1825–1877, SIA; [JH] to [ADB], [1853], actually ca. July 14, 1853, ADBP.

7. This and the following paragraph are based on Rhees, *Journals*, pp. 705, 708; JH to Richard Rush, July 15, 1853, Richard Rush Papers, Smithson Bequest, Princeton University Library.

8. Spencer F. Baird to George P. Marsh, November 14, 1853, Spencer F. Baird Private Papers, SIA.

9. JH to ADB, October 17, 1853, JH-ADB; Spencer Baird to George P. Marsh, November 14, 1853, Spencer F. Baird Private Papers, SIA.

10. Rhees, *Journals*, pp. 707–708.

11. Rhees, *Journals*, pp. 94, 98.

12. Rhees, *Journals*, pp. 91–92; JH to Asa Gray, January 10, 1853, Gray Herbarium, Harvard University.

13. JH to James N. Rix, February 21, 1853, New Hampshire Historical Society; JH to S. F. Haven, April 14, 1853, American Antiquarian Society.

14. Spencer F. Baird to George P. Marsh, February 5, 1854, Bailey Library, University of Vermont; Rufus Choate to Cabot Cushing, January 8, 1854, Chase-Forney Collection, Library of Congress; Rufus Choate to Charles C. Jewett, February 4, 1854, Houghton Library, Harvard University; Charles C. Jewett to Charles Folsom, February 9, 1854, Boston Public Library.

15. Spencer F. Baird to George P. Marsh, May 6, 1854, Bailey Library, University of Vermont.

16. JH to Joseph Leidy, March 23, 1854, Academy of Natural Sciences of Philadelphia.

17. Spencer F. Baird to George P. Marsh, May 6, 1854, Bailey Library, University of Vermont; Rhees, *Journals*, pp. 99–101, 104, 112.

18. Charles C. Jewett to George Livermore, June 15, 1854, quoted in Joseph A. Borome, *Charles Coffin Jewett* (Chicago, 1951), p. 89; Rhees, *Journals*, pp. 112–13.

19. Charles C. Jewett to Regents, July 31, 1854, JHPP; Rhees, *Journals*, pp. 114, 116–17.

20. Rhees, *Journals*, loc. cit.; JH to ADB, November 11, 1854, JH-ADB.

21. JH to ADB, November 11, 1854, JH-ADB; JH to Richard Rush, November 13, 1854, Richard Rush Papers, Smithson Bequest, Princeton University Library; JH to ADB, October 16, 1854, JH-ADB; JH Locked Book, December 2, 1854, SIA.

22. Rhees, *Journals*, p. 710.

23. Rhees, *Journals*, pp. 710–11.

24. Rhees, *Journals*, pp. 114–17.

25. Rhees, *Journals*, pp. 118–19; *The Works of Rufus Choate* (Boston, 1862), vol. I, p. 108; *Smithsonian Institution*, 33d Cong., 2d sess., H. Rept. 141 (Serial 808), March 3, 1855, pp. 64–65.

26. *Smithsonian Institution*, H. Rept. 141 (see note 25), pp. 94–95; Charles C. Jewett to Charles Folsom, April 11, 1855, Boston Public Library.

Chapter Eight

1. JH to Asa Gray, February 22, 1856, Gray Herbarium, Harvard University; Rhees, *Journals*, pp. 711–12.

2. *Annual Report of the Board of Regents of the Smithsonian Institution . . . for the year 1856* (Washington, D.C., 1857), p. 22 (cited hereafter as *Annual Report* by year date); JH to Asa Gray, April 6, 1857, Gray Herbarium, Harvard University.

3. This and the following paragraph are based on Rhees, *Journals*, p. 712.

4. JH to James H. Coffin, June 15, 1858, JH-James H. Coffin Correspondence, 1842–1873, SIA; JH to Stephen Alexander, June 24, 1858, SIA; *Annual Report 1860*, p. 53.

5. *Annual Report 1860*, p. 53; *Annual Report 1861*, p. 47.

6. JH to Spencer F. Baird, August 24, 1863, Spencer F. Baird Papers, SIA.

7. JH to ADB, August 21, 1862, JH-ADB.

8. My account of the fire is based on the testimony of those present given to a joint committee of Congress, printed as *Origin of the Fire at Smithsonian Institution*, February 21, 1865, 38th Cong., 2d sess., S. Rept. 129 (Serial 1211); JH to Louis Agassiz, January 31, 1865, William J. Rhees Papers, Huntington Library, San Marino, California; JH to John M. Stanley, March 11, 1865, SIA; JH Desk Diary, January 25, 1865, SIA.

9. JH Desk Diary, January 25, 1865, SIA.

10. JH Desk Diary, January 25, 1865, SIA.

11. This and the following paragraph are drawn from JH to Louis Agassiz, January 31, 1865, Rhees Papers; JH to John M. Stanley, March 11, 1865, SIA.

12. JH Desk Diary, January 25, 1865, SIA.

13. This and the following two paragraphs are based on JH Desk Diary, January 26, 1865, SIA; Barton S. Alexander to JH, January 25, 1865, JH Secretarial Papers, Official Incoming, SIA; JH to Louis Agassiz, January 31, 1865, Rhees

Papers; Fielding B. Meek to George H. Cook, January 29, 1865, George H. Cook Papers, Rutgers University Library; Rhees, *Journals*, pp. 235, 715; and Wilcomb E. Washburn, "Temple of the Arts," *American Institute of Architects Journal* (March 1969).

14. JH to Louis Agassiz, January 31, 1865, Rhees Papers; JH to Joseph Leidy, February 4, 1865, JH Private Letterpress, SIA.

15. JH to John Torrey, March 18, 1865, JHPP; Barton S. Alexander to JH, February 2, 1865, JH Secretarial Papers, Official Incoming, SIA; Rhees, *Journals*, p. 713.

16. Rhees, *Journals*, pp. 713–14, 717.

17. JH to Asa Gray, April 13, 1865, Gray Herbarium, Harvard University; JH to T. D. Woolsey, August 8, 1862, Woolsey Collection, Sterling Library, Yale University; JH to William H. English, January 20, 1866, William Henry Smith Memorial Library, Indiana Historical Society; JH to J. P. Lesley, March 8, 1866, American Philosophical Society.

18. JH to Salmon P. Chase, July 15, 1865, Chase-Forney Collection, Library of Congress; JH to William J. Rhees, August 17, 1865, JH Private Letterpress, SIA.

19. Rhees, *Journals*, pp. 717–18; JH to Louis Agassiz, April 20, 1867, JHPP.

20. Rhees, *Journals*, pp. 718, 720.

21. Rhees, *Journals*, p. 721.

22. Rhees, *Journals*, p. 243; JH to Asa Gray, February 28, 1866, Gray Herbarium, Harvard University.

23. Rhees, *Journals*, pp. 244–45; JH to Asa Gray, February 28, 1866, Gray Herbarium, Harvard University; JH to Asa Gray, March 8, 1867, JH Private Letterpress, SIA.

24. Rhees, *Journals*, pp. 303–304, 317.

25. Rhees, *Journals*, pp. 321–23.

26. Rhees, *Journals*, pp. 350, 354–56; JH to John Torrey, May 3, 1871, JH Private Letterpress, SIA.

27. JH to John Torrey, January 15, 1872, JH Private Letterpress, SIA.

28. JH to William H. Dall, March 13, 1872, JHPP; Rhees, *Journals*, p. 564; JH to Asa Gray, March 7, 1873, Gray Herbarium, Harvard University.

29. Rhees, *Journals*, pp. 388, 391–92, 425, 429.

30. Rhees, *Journals*, pp. 429–32.

31. *Annual Report 1875*, pp. 65, 70, 71.

32. JH to Asa Gray, January 12, 1876, Gray Herbarium, Harvard University; *Annual Report 1875*, p. 102.

33. *Annual Report 1876*, p. 120; JH to John MacLean, January 20, 1877, JH Private Letterpress, SIA.

34. National Capital Planning Commission, *Worthy of the Nation* (Washington, D.C., 1977), pp. 98–99; Tanya Edwards Beauchamp, "Adolph Cluss: An Architect in Washington during Civil War and Reconstruction," *Records of the Columbia Historical Society*, vol. 48, 1971–1972, pp. 338–58; and Daniel D. Reiff, *Washington Architecture 1791–1861: Problems in Development* (Washington, D.C., 1971), pp. 110–12.

35. JH to Asa Gray, February 15, 1877, Gray Herbarium, Harvard University; *Annual Report 1876*, p. 13.
36. *Annual Report 1876*, pp. 13, 47; JH to John MacLean, February 15, 1877, JH Private Letterpress, SIA.
37. This and the following paragraph are drawn from JH to Asa Gray, February 15, 1877, and *Annual Report 1876*, p. 13.
38. *Annual Report 1878*, p. 9; *Annual Report 1879*, p. 70; on the United States National Museum Building, see James M. Goode, "The Arts and Industries Building," in *1876: A Centennial Exhibition*, ed. Robert C. Post (Washington, D.C., 1976), pp. 206–213.

A Note on the Sources

Any investigation of the origin of the Smithsonian Institution and its building must begin with the Smithsonian Institution Archives; inside the edifice now known as the Arts and Industries Building (originally the United States National Museum) are the Joseph Henry Papers, the Alexander Dallas Bache Papers, the Spencer Fullerton Baird Papers, the Records of the National Institute, and the extant competition drawings for the Smithsonian by John Notman, Owen G. Warren, Isaiah Rogers, and James Renwick, Jr.

Next door in the Castle, Dr. Nathan Reingold and his staff are currently engaged in the publication of *The Papers of Joseph Henry*. They have generously shared with me the fruits of their exhaustive search for Henry material from other archival sources. A complete listing of these would duplicate information found above in the notes; the most important collections for the purposes of this study were the Asa Gray Papers at the Gray Herbarium of Harvard University, the John Torrey Papers at the New York Botanical Garden Library, and the Richard Rush Papers at the Princeton University Library.

Other important primary documents include the 1841 plans of Robert Mills for the Smithsonian / National Institute Building, in the Cartographic Records Section of the National Archives; the 1840 Alexander Jackson Davis plan for the Smithsonian Institution, in the Metropolitan Museum of Art, New York; and the correspondence of Robert Dale Owen and David Dale Owen, at the Workingmen's Institute, New Harmony, Indiana.

The Smithsonian Institution itself has published many of the documents concerning its establishment. One of the most crucial volumes for this study has been the minutes of the Smithsonian Board of Regents, the Executive Committee, and the Building Committee, which appeared as *The Smithsonian Institution: Journals of the Board of Regents, Reports of Committees, Etc.* (Washington, D.C., 1879). The editor of that volume, William J. Rhees, also culled all relevant material from the *Congressional Globe* to make *The Smithsonian Institution: Documents Relative to Its Origin and History* (Washington, D.C., 1879). The *Annual Reports of the Board of Regents of the Smithsonian Institution* to the United States Congress are also of use.

Many of those involved in the organization of the Smithsonian and those who knew the Renwicks left diaries, memoirs, or autobiographies. They include John Quincy Adams, James K. Polk, Philip Hone, George Templeton Strong, Charles Wilkes, Isaiah Rogers, John B. Jervis, William Campbell Preston, and Edward Sabine Renwick. All but the last of these have been published; Edward Renwick, brother of the architect, entitled his reminiscences *The Renwicks*; this work is preserved in the Local History and Genealogy Division of the New York Public Library.

Several contemporary books or pamphlets are noteworthy. Central to this study is Robert Dale Owen, *Hints on Public Architecture* (New York, 1849; reprint ed. New York, 1978), which is the clearest statement of the theory behind the Smithsonian Building. Important to Owen, his brother David Dale Owen, and Joseph Henry was Charles Lyell, *Travels in North America, in the Years 1841–2* (New York, 1845). The broadside by David Henry Arnot, *Animadversions on the Proceedings of the Regents of the Smithsonian Institution in Their Choice of an Architect . . .* (New York, 1847), contains not only an attack on the competition and the style of architecture chosen, but also the early correspondence of the Owen brothers on the building.

The formation of the Smithsonian has been recounted in a number of studies. A chronological approach is used by A. Hunter Dupree in *Science in the Federal Government* (Cambridge, Mass., 1957), and extensive use of primary sources distinguishes two essays by Wilcomb E. Washburn, "Joseph Henry's Conception of the Purpose of the Smithsonian Institution," in *A Cabinet of Curiosities*, ed. Walter Muir Whitehill (Charlottesville, 1967), and "The Influence of the Smithsonian Institution on Intellectual Life in Mid-Nineteenth-Century Washington," in *Records of the Columbia Historical Society* (Washington, D.C., 1963–65). On the history of the District of Columbia, the two volumes of Constance McLaughlin Green, *Washington: A History of the Capital 1800–1950* (Princeton, 1962), remain unparalleled.

For many years, architectural historians glossed over the period of the Gothic Revival in America. Fortunately, this is no longer so. James Early, *Romanticism and American Architecture* (New York, 1965), is quite good on the era, as is the somewhat deceptively titled *Changing Ideals in Modern Architecture 1750–1950*, by Peter Collins (London and Montreal, 1965). Two volumes in the Johns Hopkins Studies in Nineteenth-Century Architecture series have raised the standard of scholarship in the period: Phoebe B. Stanton, *The Gothic Revival and American Church Architecture: An Episode in Taste 1840–1856* (Baltimore, 1968), and George L. Hersey's intriguing—if somewhat kinky—*High Victorian Gothic: A Study in Associationism* (Baltimore, 1972). William H. Pierson's volume II-A of *American Buildings and Their Architects*, interminably subtitled *Technology and the Picturesque, The Corporate and the Early Gothic Styles* (Garden City, 1978), includes a chapter on James Renwick, Jr., and St. Patrick's Cathedral, one of the best published essays on Renwick to date.

On the Smithsonian Building itself, several recent works stand out. Daniel D. Reiff, in *Washington Architecture 1791–1861: Problems in Development* (Washington, D.C., 1971) devotes a chapter to the Washington work of James Renwick, Jr., and A. J. Downing. Also of prime importance is Cynthia Field's introduction to the 1978 Da Capo Press reprint edition of Robert Dale Owen's *Hints on Public Architecture*. A remarkable source book for the study of Washington architecture is James M. Goode, *Capital Losses: A Cultural History of Washington's Destroyed Buildings* (Washington, D.C., 1979). All of these studies have been quite influential on the present work.

Index